REAL
STEPS
TO
ENLIGHTENMENT

About the Author

Amy Elizabeth Garcia is a Reiki master who receives guidance from her angels, healing guides, and the Master Jesus as she channels the Christ Force energy. She teaches workshops and conducts intuitive counseling and healing sessions.

REAL STEPS

TO
ENLIGHTENMENT

*Dynamic Tools
to Create Change*

Amy Elizabeth Garcia

Llewellyn Publications
Woodbury, Minnesota

First Edition
First Printing, 2006

Book design and layout by Joanna Willis
Cover design by Lisa Novak
Cover image © Comstock
Editing by Jane Hilken

Llewellyn is a registered trademark of Llewellyn Worldwide, Ltd.

Library of Congress Cataloging-in-Publication Data
Garcia, Amy Elizabeth.
    Real steps to enlightenment: dynamic tools to create change / Amy Elizabeth Garcia.
        p.   cm.
    ISBN-13: 978-0-7387-0896-6
    ISBN-10: 0-7387-0896-8
    1. Spiritual life. 2. Change—Religious aspects. I. Title.

BL624.G355 2006
299'.93—dc22

2006041022

Llewellyn Publications
A Division of Llewellyn Worldwide, Ltd.
2143 Wooddale Drive, Dept. 0-7387-0896-8
Woodbury, MN 55125-2989, U.S.A.
www.llewellyn.com

To Larry, Anthony, Christopher, and Briana
for giving me unconditional love

contents

acknowledgments

I extend thanks to the talented staff at Llewellyn Worldwide, Ltd. for all of their hard work bringing this book into publication. I would like to acknowledge Jane Hilken and Nanette Peterson for their editing and assistance. I am grateful for the lovely book layout by Joanna Willis and the luminous cover design by Lisa Novak. I would also like to thank Evelyn of Enlightenment for her encouragement during the writing of the manuscript. I appreciated the efforts of Michele Haviland and Linda Reneau in helping me to prepare the document for submission. A special thanks to Cyndi Butler for twenty years of friendship and inspiration. Finally, I would like to express gratitude to all of the practitioners and friends connected with www.spiritualawarenessnetwork.org. I know you will continue to spread light, healing, and peace in the world.

introduction

Some people on a spiritual path are overwhelmed with the many teachings and doctrines that promise enlightenment or God-realization. This book is a tool to help you go within for your own higher guidance and find the answers you seek. By breaking down the process into easily attainable steps, the journey will be made easier. I found my life improving when I connected with my guides and angels. They were instrumental in writing this book, and I appreciate all of the help that I have received from Spirit. This project has been a major source of instruction for my own growth and development.

I have studied metaphysics for over fifteen years and have a great passion for anything that gives me a greater understanding of the worlds beyond our senses. The exciting part of this exploration has been the real-life application of the principles and tools I discovered. I have gained a stronger connection to the Unseen through firsthand experiences.

Over the years, I have explored many spiritual practices, however, I never delved into the arenas of channeling or spirit communication. I suppose that my childhood conditioning had made me wary of experimenting with these techniques. I waited until I found a teacher that I trusted completely. I participated in a spirit communication class, and my guides and angels came through very quickly and easily. I am glad that I took this step into the unknown because I have gained useful information and support from these communications.

An entity from the causal plane named Jahallah was my main contact during the writing of this book. Beings who dwell on this level of reality have completed their spiritual lessons and no longer need to incarnate on earth. They continue their work as guides and teachers to those who are still making the journey back home. Some teachers on this plane have never had bodies. I am glad that Jahallah had lifetimes on earth because his experiences were easy to relate to, and his advice was applicable to real-life situations. I believe I connected with Jahallah because our goals and energies resonated with each other. We worked together as a team for our mutual evolution and growth.

Even Jahallah's name had significance to me. If you break his name into two parts, the "Jah" is an abbreviation for the biblical Jehovah. "Allah," of course, is the deity of the Koran. During one session, Jahallah said, "I am your reminder that the God of Israel and of Islam are the same. There is no separation in the One." I searched for his name on the Internet, but only found a song with a similar title. It was about ending division and warfare. The lyrics encouraged people to let go of the barriers and prejudices that separate them in order to create peace. This was quite amazing to me because the incidents surrounding 9/11 were a major catalyst that motivated me to move forward on my spiritual path.

I also received help on this project from the angels. I have always had a deep love for the angelic realm. I know that our lives can be made much easier when we call upon our angels for assistance. This was a recurring theme in my channeled communications. My spirit helpers really wanted to emphasize that it is important to utilize the help that is readily available to us at all times. There are many angels, and they all have unique gifts to share. When I would bring through prayers from the angels, I could sense their energetic qualities, such as gratitude, encouragement, or synergy. I would play a guessing game to see if I could determine what angel was coming through.

I sat at my computer each morning and did a meditation to create a channeling connection. I was in a conscious state when I received information. Many times I had to control my desire to edit what was coming through. When I trusted the process, the ideas would flow. The anecdotes from Jahallah's earth lives reminded me of biblical parables. I would reread them and find many underlying meanings.

We are all on different paths, but our destination is the same. Deep within each of us is the desire to reconnect with the Divine. Jahallah and I developed thirty-three chapters to help people move forward on their spiritual journeys. Each topic covers aspects of life or qualities that we aspire to create, such as joy, safety, healing, and harmony.

Sometimes we get so busy just surviving this earth life that we forget to notice the subtle lessons that can be found in our daily experiences. If we embrace and accept the gifts, we will have richer and more fulfilling journeys. However, enlightenment cannot be found by reading a book. The purpose of this book is to be a catalyst to motivate you to take the steps necessary to move forward on your own path. You can read it from beginning to end or open it at random for daily guidance.

Each chapter is divided into four sections. The first is Jahallah's message. He provides spiritual insights and gives examples of how they can work. The second section is a personal story from my own life that illustrates these concepts in action and how those experiences helped me to grow. A few of my friends and colleagues contributed stories from their own lives as well. The third section is a prayer inspired by the angels. I have included this part as a reminder to connect with the spiritual realms for support. There is tremendous power in prayer and our words and thoughts have a great impact on what we create. By teaming up with our unseen helpers, this power is amplified.

The final section of each chapter is perhaps the most important. It is the part that you write. I challenge you to think of three ways to bring these qualities of Spirit into your own daily experiences. The four sections of each chapter will help you implement positive change in your life through utilizing divinely guided (1) Information, (2) Inspiration, (3) Intention, and (4) Action. It is my hope that you will not just read this book and put it on the shelf. Instead, I hope it will inspire you to use what you have learned, set personal goals, and take steps to move closer to enlightenment.

Love and Blessings,
Amy Garcia

purpose

The great and glorious masterpiece of humanity is to know how to live with a purpose.

MONTAIGNE

One of the most important questions that people ask themselves is, "Why am I here?" They wonder what their purpose is for being on this planet. There are as many answers to that question as there are individuals who ask it. Everyone has innate gifts and abilities that can provide service to mankind. Don't make answering this question a struggle. Finding your mission can be as easy as following your heart, developing your talents and doing what comes naturally. There are many aspects of our lives on earth that shape and mold us on different levels. We learn from relationships, the environment, our livelihoods, and universal laws.

Your soul chose to incarnate here in order to experience diversity and evolution. Earth is a place where you encounter duality— hot and cold, up and down, good and bad. Although these perceptions are not real in Truth, they provide a training ground for

1

self-discovery. Sometimes the quickest way to discover who you are is to experience who you are not. Through overcoming the challenges presented to us in our everyday activities, we tap into our inner resources of Divine intelligence and power.

If you are reading this book, it is highly probable that you are on a lightworker's mission. You are here to realize your full potential and to help others do the same. It is possible to eliminate limitations and negative emotions in order to have a direct relationship with the Source. This connection is always available to us. We only need to remove the blocks and obstacles we have placed in front of our vision. As you look around you, it seems that there is much to heal in your world. There is a lot of work to do. Healing is not a quest for the faint of heart. It will take dedication and a readiness to live in a different way. You will need to make spiritual growth a top priority.

People on earth invest a lot of energy in obligations, commitments, and responsibilities. Who is creating these obligations? Is it your ego self or your higher self? Busyness and excessive activities may keep you distracted from going within and connecting with your true purpose or soul contracts. You don't really have to worry about finding your life mission, because it will find you. People and circumstances are drawn to you so that you might work through your karmic lessons and have opportunities to extend love. You will be guided to situations that will enable you to accomplish the work you were sent here to do.

Wishing for things to take place in a certain manner needs to be accompanied by action. Too frequently people get lost in study and contemplation, yet do little on the earthly plane to bring their goals into manifestation. Bringing forth channeled information is one way to take action and create a wealth of information that will be useful to yourself and others. Your purpose on earth is to find ways to express love and exchange energy for the ascension of mankind. As you meet each person in your daily activities, remember that it is a holy encounter.

We see our inner selves reflected in those around us. If you find yourself in a situation that is unsettling, go within to regain your balance and shift your perceptions. Give your blessings to the "teachers" you see all around you. You are all here to help each other evolve. There are souls who have completed their missions on earth and who exist in the spiritual realms. They are ready to assist those who are still on the planet. I dwell on the causal plane with others who are doing work to uplift and heal mankind. We see more clearly on this side of the veil and know that evolution is taking place at a rapid pace. I have incarnated many times and I understand the dynamics of the human experience.

While living in your world, the Master Jesus saw the Divine spark within everyone. In doing so, He created miracles and each person's fears, doubts, illnesses, and illusions fell away instantly. Take a moment to look in the mirror and see yourself through God's eyes. Imagine the faults and imperfections just falling away. Energy follows intention. This is not a game of "pretend"; this is a game of "being real." The more you learn to direct your thoughts, imagination, and creativity in positive ways, the more you will see your dreams coming true and your soul's purpose becoming clear.

You have developed a strong conduit for bringing spiritual information and healing to the planet. When you ask for assistance, *it will be provided. Your guides will not invade your personal energy field. You are in control of these communications and we are here to help when called upon. With practice, you will be able to maintain the channel effortlessly. You will receive guidance from your Higher Self and you will know what to do next. Take action today to manifest the life you desire. You are in my heart and soul, dear one, Jahallah.*

Sometimes we find our purpose after years of searching. Sometimes the Universe gets our attention quickly. My friend, Marisa Ryan, had an abrupt awakening that guided her into a career as a medium. Her mother died of a heart attack immediately following a Thanksgiving dinner, and her niece was found dead in her bedroom from unknown causes two days later. Marisa found herself wanting answers about life, death, and life after death. She read many books that led her to astral traveling to visit her deceased mother and niece. She soon came to realize that she could communicate with them whenever she wanted.

Then one night she was on her computer. She was reading her e-mails when the spirit of a girl who had been killed appeared in front of her. She showed Marisa many details of her murder and begged for help. The next day Marisa called the police and told them what she had learned. They wanted to meet with Marisa because they thought she had something to do with the crime.

The deceased girl told other spirits that Marisa could see and hear them, and she began seeing and hearing spirits all around her. They came to her desperately wanting to convey messages to their families. Marisa took a few classes to learn how to control her gift and began giving messages from the other side for many people. She also began to work with the detectives on their cases. Within six months, she had become a professional psychic medium. She now does hundreds of readings, regularly speaks on the radio, and teaches classes in spirit communication. She feels truly blessed to be able to help grieving families and their loved ones.

Like many people, I have wondered what I am supposed to do with my life. I did well in school and pursued various careers, but nothing seemed to inspire me. I attended college for a few years, but never found what I was looking for. I explored social work, but after being a houseparent at a group home, I found that I wasn't really cut out for that stressful occupation. I was very emotional and tried to solve other people's problems. When I learned that I could help people most by sharing personal growth tools that have worked for me, I was more effective in creating change. My sensitivity proved to be an asset in my healing and counseling sessions, but I encouraged people to create their own solutions to life's challenges.

Writing this book felt like something that I needed to do. I was very uplifted when I worked on this project. The fact that the subject matter teaches tools for spiritual growth felt right as well. I think that my purpose during this lifetime is to be a messenger and a person who brings people together for growth and healing. Organizing, coordinating, and communicating come naturally to me, so I like to plan events and network for the metaphysical community. I didn't create it that way, but when I did these things, everything seemed to be in Divine order. Your purpose may or may not be tied into your career. However, since the majority of our time is spent working, our lives have more vitality and greater rewards if we truly enjoy what we are doing.

Let go of external judgments about your life situation and pay more attention to how it feels. You can have all of the trappings of success, but still remain unfulfilled. It took me a long time to feel like I was succeeding, despite external circumstances. The years that I have spent following my heart have been the most rewarding of my life.

I did feel it was part of my life purpose to give birth to my children, but as they grew older I knew that there was more to the plan. Recently, I set out to find myself again—to remember what I am supposed to do. I don't have all the details worked out, but my instincts are guiding me. The pieces started to fall into place when I dedicated myself fully to my spiritual path. Finding your "mission" shouldn't be difficult. Life has a way of unfolding and guiding you into the right place at the right time.

It is true that many of us take painful detours along the way, but we can always get back on track. If you are at peace with yourself, you are probably headed in the right direction. If you are depressed or miserable, examine your life for the root cause of your problems and take action to make changes. Don't be too hard on yourself in the process. You might not think that you are fulfilling your purpose because your life is not glamorous or eventful. A mother feeding her children, a student gaining knowledge, or a person collecting the garbage are exactly where they need to be. We each have to take the necessary steps to prepare ourselves for our unique path.

Discovering your purpose is facilitated by self-exploration. Realize what parts of yourself are in need of healing. Find out what gifts and abilities you have that will help others. By exploring various aspects of your life, such as the issues covered in this book, you start to create the life that is perfect for you. For example, think of what brings you joy, peace, encouragement, harmony, understanding, and sanctuary. In what ways can you follow your heart to create adventure, celebration, clarity, release, and transformation? Your purpose will begin to take shape as you bring these various aspects into focus and create a holistic experience designed especially for you.

I think that we are here on this planet in order to more fully understand who we are. Through limitations and challenges, we can experience who we are not. When we rise above difficulties, we remember who we are as powerful spiritual beings. We live in a world of seeming duality, but this illusion falls away as we dig deeper. We will find love and perfection underneath any block to God's presence. When everything we do honors universal principles, life, and love, it is impossible to fail in our purpose. The final aspect of this process is to help others do the same.

Jesus the Christ overcame the limitations of this world and taught that anyone could do what he did. He had mastered many spiritual gifts, including healing and clairvoyance. My explorations into the world of metaphysics have taught me that we all can develop the abilities that the Master possesses.

As you read the stories in this book, you will learn how psychic information has helped me. I have had many positive experiences as I received guidance from my talented colleagues. However, I do not have a dependence on them because I know I am responsible for my own life, choices, and growth. We are all teachers and students, helping each other to remember our true selves. There is a saying that you will "get to heaven by holding the hand of the person behind you." When we eliminate beliefs in separation and understand that what we do for others, we do for ourselves, we make great strides toward finding our purpose.

Angel of Purpose Prayer

"Mother-Father God, my divine purpose is becoming clear to me. I encounter the perfect people and situations along my journey that enable me to fulfill my mission. I am willing to take Spirit-directed action in order to bring healing and love to the world. I am grateful for my spiritual guides and helpers that assist me along the way. My goal is to reunite with my Source and create heaven on earth. I accept the abundant flow of love that carries me toward my goal. And so it is."

Three ways that I will experience purpose in my life are . . .

1.

2.

3.

IDEAS:

1. Use tools for self-discovery, for example, personality and aptitude tests, meditation, journaling.

2. Work on developing burgeoning talents.

3. Explore new career options.

joy

When you follow your bliss . . . doors will open
where you would not have thought there would be
doors.

JOSEPH CAMPBELL

The cosmos is made up of ever-changing energy particles that resulted from the One. It is fascinating to watch the evolution of
matter and consciousness. You are on an inward journey as well
as an outward one. What you create within will be manifested in
your external world. Changes come when we release the patterns
from the past that no longer serve you.

What areas of your life would you like to improve? What blocks
do you find in the way of achieving your goals? They are self-cre-
ated. You can release them effortlessly. Bringing light into your life
is not difficult. It just requires willingness. Changing the way you
think about a situation is the surest way to create peace in your life.
As you look for the good in each experience, all heaviness will lift.

When I was a young man in a past incarnation, my father raised
me to be a printer. I was his apprentice and learned all about the

trade. My name was Josap, and I gained recognition in this field. I printed news bulletins and trade papers. I became a source for news in the community because I had access to so much information.

One day, I was approached by a lady who was dressed in a grand fashion. She wanted to know about palatial estates for sale in the area. There were not many to choose from, but I gave her the postings that I had on file. She engaged me in conversation about the mysteries of life. She asked me questions, and I provided her with many answers. During that lifetime, I had heard so many stories that I had learned what worked and what didn't.

She came to me regularly and treated me like a wise mystic. She told her friends about our talks, and they started to come to me as well. She knew that I was hard-pressed for funds at my print shop, so she donated generous amounts of money to help me in my work. She encouraged me to write down my ideas and print them so that I could share the wisdom with others.

I proceeded to print a weekly publication filled with spiritual guidance and anecdotes. People in the community contributed stories. This became a tool for drawing people together and inciting passion about living a Spirit-filled life. I gained great joy from this project and it prospered. It made me stop and realize that when we follow our joy, everything we need is provided.

Your burdens will become lighter as you follow your heart. Go within and ask yourself what your ideal life would be like. Believe that you can reach your dreams and take action each day toward achieving them. If anything becomes a struggle, you may want to change your focus. Life can flow with ease and grace when you are in alignment with your true calling. If you are encountering

obstacles, look for ways to extend yourself in light to others. Fol-
low your joy. It will always lead you in the right direction. Na-
maste. Jahallah.

I know from personal experience that Jahallah's words are true. I was employed as a speech and language assistant at a local elementary school. I enjoyed working with the children, and I used my skills in new and creative ways. I was happiest when I managed the department on my own and designed lesson plans. The positive energy of that experience ended just as I was approached with the opportunity to coordinate spiritual renewal festivals for a local metaphysical center. I spent so much time on these projects that it seemed appropriate to leave my job. After several months, the financial implications of this decision started to impact my life.

I began an extensive job search, seeking employment with the city and county hospitals and universities. I would follow up on any notices for office administrators that were posted in the local newspapers. However, every time I had to put on those uncomfortable interview outfits and high heels, my heart would sink. I told myself that I had to "do the right thing" and get a "real" job. I couldn't be irresponsible! This had been a recurring theme in my life. I always took responsibilities very seriously and didn't want to let anyone down. In fact, in my high school journalism class, I had the honor of being voted "most dependable" and "most responsible." Those were unusual accolades for a teenager. Over the years, I have really had to shift my perspective and live life less seriously. As I was turning forty, I had yet another reminder that life flows easily when we follow our joy.

I got turned down for so many jobs that I was starting to question myself. I knew I could handle any of those positions blindfolded, so why was I finding so many closed doors? After many of the interviews, I would stop by a local metaphysical store to drop off flyers and chat with the owner. The store owner had created a spiritual oasis filled with beautiful merchandise and books. I met her at a festival that I had coordinated. She was interested in working with me and utilizing my networking and organizational skills in her business. However, since the store had just opened, she did not know if she was in a financial position to hire an extra person. Also, I wasn't sure if the part-time income would be sufficient to maintain my family's lifestyle.

The Universe made the decision for us. Her family commitments created the need for assistance managing the store. Her grandmother was ill and moved into her house. She also needed to spend a lot of time with her psychic son, who was the reason she embarked on this venture. I was returning from yet another unsuccessful job interview when she made me the offer again. I was finally ready to release this futile mission to find a "real job" and embrace what I would enjoy.

When I let go of what I "should" do, what I really wanted manifested. The store was five minutes away from home and a convenient setting for my healing work. I would continue to coordinate programs and provide networking services for the community. I would have the mornings free to work on my writing projects, and I could maintain a balanced family life. I received another reminder that the journey that brings us closer to enlightenment can be painless and pleasurable. Every step forward is another opportunity to follow our joy.

Angel of Joy Prayer

"Mother-Father God, I welcome the essence of joy that helps me to realize the desires of my heart. I will extend this gift so that others will be blessed. I know that genuine acceptance of "what is" will create happiness in my life. I see the value in each experience. I know that beauty is all around me. As I follow my joy, all good will come to me. I make a joyful noise and give praises to my Creator for my life. And so it is."

Three ways that I will experience joy in my life are . . .

1.

2.

3.

IDEAS:

1. Swim in the ocean.

2. Send out a resume for a job that sounds fun.

3. Watch a child discover something new.

trust

Put all your faith in the Love of God within you;
eternal, changeless and forever unfailing. This is
the answer to whatever confronts you today.

A COURSE IN MIRACLES

*Circumstances change. They are transient and not indicative of
what is ultimately true. Have you ever wished that things were
fundamentally different in your life? Once you lift the veil of illusion, the truth that is underneath will astound you. Don't be discouraged if you think that you are experiencing hardship. Your
trust in your Creator and your innate abilities to manifest unlimited abundance will see you through the difficult times.*

*I know that you are wondering what to do differently to make
things change. First, you can take time to generate feelings of
trust and faith. At first you may feel like you are "mustering up"
these qualities. With practice, they will become part of your energy field and affect your creative process accordingly. Things will
flow more smoothly and you will witness your dreams becoming
your reality.*

17

It will be nearly impossible for your life to change if you hold onto beliefs such as "life is hard" or "the world is an unsafe place" or "people are out to get me." When you hold onto those energies, that is what you will experience. It is true that some choices in our lives could bring us harm, but the greatest detriment to ourselves is living in a state of fear. If your intentions are high and you are in connection with your Higher Guidance, you will be led to safe places. Immersing yourself in a fear consciousness will only lead you down the wrong paths. Trust that you will be cared for and guided into right action.

When I was a teenager on earth, I had an experience that taught me about trust. I was bathing in a river, and a water snake came floating down with the current. My friend and I were looking for game to make a stew for our dinner, and I thought this might be a tasty addition. I was not familiar with all of the varieties of snakes, and some dangerous breeds looked very similar to the harmless ones. I wasn't sure what to do. I didn't have any hunting tools within reach. I would need to grab the snake as it floated by. I probably wouldn't have taken the risk, but a loud voice inside of me guided me to take the chance. I alerted my friend on the shore, and I flung the snake toward him. He had a stake ready and was safely able to procure our meal.

We have chosen to share this message with you today because many on the planet are experiencing loss. We commend you for keeping your foremost priority on maintaining your peace and continuing to trust in the providence of the Universe. We are presented with challenges at times in order for us to strengthen these qualities within us. Take time to relax now and let those positive *beliefs filter throughout every fiber of your being, strengthening your convictions.*

You cannot be separate from God, no matter how things appear. Sometimes the distance appears so great that it seems impossible to find your way back. You are safe and cared for, and you will find the answers you need. People create very complex scenarios in their lives to test this. It only takes an instant; it is a journey without distance. God's presence is within you and all around you. Just brush the specks from your eyes so that you can see clearly. Remove the negative emotions from your heart so that you can feel love strongly. Rid yourself of limiting beliefs so that you can know Truth.

Dear one, you are so loved and cherished. Don't identify yourself with your human foibles, but with your Divine presence. You were created in the image and likeness of God. You are holy and perfect. As you remember this, it will be reflected in your outer circumstances. Have trust in this one thing, and it will be so. Heartfelt encouragement, Jahallah.

Jahallah gave me this message on a day when my husband's work truck was robbed. When times are hard, we sometimes start to wonder, "Why is this happening? What am I doing wrong?" I knew this pattern of thinking would be unproductive, so I renewed my commitment to trusting in the universal plan. All of the stolen tools were replaced easily and effortlessly.

Over the years, I have come to see how much our beliefs impact our lives. Before learning spiritual principles about prosperity, I lived in a very fear-based consciousness of lack. This quickly manifested in my day-to-day experiences. Early in our marriage, I was caring for three small children and my husband was working for a company that paid a fraction of the industry standard even though he was a great asset to his employer. I was staying at home with the kids and working at unpleasant part-time jobs. I drove a beat-up '56 Chevy that had a penchant for breaking down in intersections. I had no clue that I was creating these dynamics by my lack of trust and my limiting beliefs.

I got hit in the head with the proverbial two-by-four one afternoon as I drove up to the ATM. I was thinking, "I have to check the balance of my account to see if any checks have bounced." I accessed a "quick statement" only to realize that the one-dollar fee for this service had created insufficient funds for my outstanding check. Through many similar tearful and frustrating episodes, I gained more of an understanding of how the Universe works. What we think and believe is going to be given to us. Our lives will only change externally when we change from within.

There is more than enough for everyone on the planet. Abundance can take on many forms and be given to you through many different channels. For example, you don't always need money as a means for exchange. We have a wonderful system of bartering in the metaphysical community that allows us to enjoy those services and luxuries we might not always be able to afford. Opportunities for homes, clothing, services, food, travel, and entertainment can also be given as gifts from the Universe. I remember one incident that occurred years after I had left a life of lack and hardship behind me. I had taken my car to a mechanic for repair. It was a recurring problem and I was almost ready to start the "why me?" syndrome. I got a quick reality check.

I admit that on the day I brought my car back into the shop, I was a little misty-eyed because my son had been in an accident, and we were restructuring our lives to accommodate his needs. I was between jobs and dressed in a sweltering polyester outfit for another stressful interview. I really didn't feel up to handling one more problem or expense. The owner of the shop was a friendly Middle Eastern man. He asked me what was wrong, and I briefly shared my hard-luck story.

He told me, "Don't worry about the car. I will fix it free of charge. When times are hard, people need to help each other out." I was overwhelmed with gratitude. This man hardly knew me, but he was willing to help me out in my time of need. This incident certainly added some luster to my current worldview and helped me to maintain my trust.

I believe in what Carolyn Myss calls "grace bank accounts." Keep making deposits into it by being of service to others, and your energy will be returned to you. I caution total dependence on the "kindness of strangers," however, as it will lead to disempowerment. Planning to win the state lottery is also probably not the best game plan either. I did an intuitive reading for a friend one day, and the cards indicated an unexpected source of money in his future. He thought that might mean that the father who had abandoned him thirty years ago might reappear and make financial amends. I was more inclined to believe that a better job might become available, but the Universe has a way of surprising us in times of crisis.

Life, to me, is a continual exchange of energies. What you put out, you get back. The easiest way to have trust that you will be sustained by the Universe is simply to do your best. Eliminate fear-based thinking and *know* that you are divinely protected and cared for. We are infinite beings made in the image and likeness of God. All we need to do is eliminate the veils that are blocking our view of our true self. We live in a world of pure potential, and there is every reason to trust that it is good.

Angel of Trust Prayer

"Mother-Father God, I have trust that everything is planned in a way that supports my highest good. I am secure in knowing that the world is a safe and wonderful place. I will hold that vision and help others to realize the perfection of creation. I dedicate my life to eliminating fear, separation, and limiting beliefs. When I encounter challenges, I will find the lesson and move forward. I trust that my choices will be guided by Divine inspiration and that I will realize success. And so it is."

Three ways that I will experience trust in my life are . . .

1.

2.

3.

IDEAS:

1. Create a positive affirmation such as "I trust that the Universe is supporting me in manifesting the life of my dreams."

2. Take a chance with an extreme sport like white-water rafting or skydiving.

3. Give something away with no concern about lack.

body care

The truth of the matter is that you always know
the right thing to do. The hard part is doing it.

GENERAL H. NORMAN SCHWARZKOPF

You will raise your vibration through physical and spiritual techniques. Jesus began his journey on this earth by making preparations for encompassing large amounts of energy in order to bring forth healing and wisdom. Other mystics, yogis, and spiritual teachers have done the same. You can do this by modifying your diet and exercise regime. Drink plenty of water and eat foods that are high in vibration. Spirit communication is an activity that requires focus and concentration.

Begin by knowing that Spirit is available to assist you in all aspects of your life. Channeled information comes to you at different times during the day, urging you to make decisions based on your own highest good. Believe that the perfect communication will come through at appropriate times. Spirit communication is going to be a large part of your contribution to others. Many times in the past you have felt separate. You discovered what it feels like without the remembrance of the Light. I know you have felt a deeper sense of peace and comfort. Congratulations on passing from one realm of awareness to another.

It is time to step up the vibration of your physical body. You have noticed that when you perform intuitive counseling or healing work, you show signs of releasing blocks and density. Continue to take action toward developing your physical vehicle to a level that will enable Spirit to make contact easily. I know that as you make progress in this area, the benefits will be great. Would you make a commitment to engage in one hour of physical activity each day? Others would suggest less time because people have difficulty carving out large blocks of time from their busy schedules. However, the dedication will be necessary to achieve the desired results.

When I was on the planet, manual labor was an integral part of our daily lives, so obesity wasn't a big problem. We put out so much energy growing our food that we needed all of the sustenance we could get. However, I remember one time when my sister had baked a pastry filled with sugar and fat. We sat there eating every last morsel and unfortunately felt very sick afterwards. We were wondering if the temporary satisfaction was worth the aftermath of discomfort. It is important to listen to the signals that your body is giving you. Eliminating alcohol and other toxic substances from your diet will enable your body to perform at its optimum ability.

When your body becomes healthy, it is a better transmitter for spiritual frequencies. It is true that some foods can limit your perception of high-frequency signals from your spiritual helpers. A healthy body will help you transmit more life force in healing work. What are your reasons for improving your health and physical appearance? Is it to receive admiration from others in order to feel good about yourself? If you approach this venture with an attitude of not being good enough, you will be in a self-defeating cycle. Begin by knowing that you are perfect and that you are just letting go of any blocks that are obscuring that vision.

I know that there are many reasons people seek solace in food and chemical substances. Some try to fill a void and some try to dull a pain. I would encourage you to go directly to the source of the issue to heal it. If you are bored or lack companionship, write out a game plan to change the situation. When people are involved in uplifting activities that bring them joy, overindulgence is forgotten. If you are feeling a lack of love in your life, go within to find it. Spiritual masters, such as Jesus, can extend loving energy to elevate people. Pray to receive a boost, not by toxic stimulants, but by love.

I know that you have tried to succeed in matters of diet and exercise in the past. You have become frustrated by "failures." One thing you can do differently this time is to ask for a team of health angels and guides to support you. You will be given motivation, reminders, promptings, and guidance to direct you on a healthful path. You now know that I am with you always and would never forsake you. Begin each day with a prayer of gratitude for this experience. Go forth in a state of peace and extend your light to others. Blessings and adoration, Jahallah.

This message was yet another reminder that diet and exercise played an important role in my overall mind-body-spirit development. When I purchased a package of angel oracle cards, I found two body care cards. Was somebody up there trying to tell me something? It is true that after giving birth to twins, my body was in need of restoration. Even when my twins were ten years old, people would think that I was pregnant because my stomach was so distended. I rededicated myself to creating health in order to be a better channel for energy work.

It's a good thing that I found alternative healing, because I have a great aversion to going to the doctor. When I finally had to see a physician about a rash on my arm, she became alarmed that my blood pressure was high. She gave me a prescription for medication that made me feel very uncomfortable. I discontinued the medication, but I continued to be proactive in solving my health issues. Fortunately, people that I had met in the metaphysical community introduced me to an M.D. who was also a psychic. He told me about the spiritual, emotional, and energetic factors influencing my health. He also did a cranial-sacral balancing technique that lowered my blood pressure by thirty points in a few minutes. He encouraged me to meditate and "run my energy" regularly to maintain a normal level.

I know that if every doctor had access to this kind of information, the world would be virtually free of dis-ease. There are many unseen influences that affect our energy fields every day. One phenomenon that I found out about was chording. Apparently, other people can "chord" us for various reasons to utilize our energy and healing abilities. I had been experiencing some discomfort on the back of my left torso, but as usual avoided seeing a doctor. One afternoon, I visited a fair at a local metaphysical shop and met a gentleman who had an aura imaging machine. The computer showed gray blotches where I was experiencing the problem.

He had a few minutes to run healing energy on the spot, but I needed a more intensive treatment. I was in terrible pain, and I contacted a psychic institute where they dealt with these kinds of issues. All of the participants in the session saw an energy chord attached to me. It took a lot of effort and concentration for them to remove the chord. They told me that there was a belief or resonance within myself that was allowing this to happen. They told me that as a healer, I had the tendency to be empathic and take on other people's issues.

It is true that I am very sensitive to energy, and I am not comfortable in certain groups of people. On occasion, I have taken on other people's issues in an attempt to help. However, this time the result was debilitating, and I had to stop the energy exchange. I have to admit that my healing was not instantaneous. I may have back-stepped for a while, not sure if I really wanted to let it go. I went to a respected psychic counselor and explored the reasons why this dynamic had taken place. There must have been something within me that was carrying those patterns and willing to accept the chord.

We worked on removing the chord, but even when it was gone, some pain still remained. It had been there so long that deterioration had taken place on the physical level. In the weeks that followed, I had healing work done on me by various practitioners. I could feel energy heating up as it worked on the damaged parts of my body. I wanted to cover all of my bases, so I went to a naturopath who did muscle testing and prescribed nutritional supplements. I did breathwork and Reiki and asked for assistance from my angels. I felt well within a few weeks. I am trying to prevent illness from occurring in my life by working with energy on many levels. We can eliminate problems in our subtle bodies before they become deeply entrenched in our physical bodies.

I have found that when I pay attention to eating healthfully and staying active, my energy is high and I am more able to attract what I want. Since my spiritual work is what motivates me, I am noticing how it is affected by my health. I would encourage you to look at what excites you in life and how it would be made better by having a strong, healthy body. I know that the temptation of instant gratification is great in our society, but the long-term benefits of wise choices are worth the effort.

Angel of Body Care Prayer

"Mother-Father God, I cherish my body and recognize its value as a temple for Spirit. I will make choices that promote my health and well-being. If I encounter challenges in these endeavors, I will call upon the support of my spiritual helpers. I will stay focused on the positive results and benefits of proper exercise and nutrition. I will take time out of my schedule to pamper myself and nurture my body. I extend gratitude to my Creator for the gift of this miraculous vessel. And so it is."

Three ways that I will experience body care in my life are . . .

1.

2.

3.

IDEAS:

1. Eat vegan for a day. Treat yourself to gourmet creations at a local restaurant to make it fun.

2. Engage in an outdoor activity, such as hiking, that connects you with the natural world.

3. Meditate and do breathing exercises.

release

> When one door of happiness closes, another
> opens; but often we look so long at the closed
> door that we do not see the one which has been
> opened for us.
>
> HELEN KELLER

Practice going within to find your center point of stillness. Ask for assistance if you have not had much experience with meditation. Please be assured that as you take steps to join with the Divine, your efforts will be rewarded. Do not be discouraged because things are not quite as you would envision them. The perfect plan for your ultimate growth is unfolding.

You are most loved and exonerated (relieved of responsibility, obligation, or hardship). Practice connecting with the Divine on a daily basis. I encourage you to continue your efforts to bring peace and union to your world. Generations of people have lived in shadow, not knowing the Truth. Misconceptions about their connection with the Divine have kept them afraid and ignorant of love's presence. God has never left you and is always available to be a source of light to help you create your holy purpose on earth.

When you release attachment to how things should look, your vision will become clear. You will feel a burden being lifted from you. You will make room for more abundance. When we hold onto expectations and limiting beliefs, there is no room for peace to enter. Have you ever noticed that when you are struggling against something, the current seems to get stronger? You are blocking the flow of life when you hold on to things.

When I was a young boy, my father took me aside one day and asked me to give him assistance with his woodworking. He showed me how to chisel the wood and fit two pieces together. I was not very adept at using tools and soon became frustrated. I tried to insert a peg into a hole and it was not working. I tried with all my might to force it. The peg splintered, and I also damaged the hole.

My father counseled me that I should have used my file to enlarge the receptacle. He told me that the wood and tools were extensions of myself. I needed to work with them instead of fighting against them. If I encountered an obstacle, I should rest a moment and wait for inspiration to solve the problem. I followed his advice and modified my approach. I was very pleased with the results.

If you find yourself fighting against something in your life, take a moment to look at it from another perspective. What might be gained if you released your "control" in the situation? Would you regain your peace and have a chance to try another path? When we hold on tightly, we create a dynamic of constriction. This can cause damage to our physical and emotional bodies. Meditation is

a good tool to "file away" debris and open your receptacle to re-
ceive something bigger and better.

There is a story about a monkey who reaches into a jar to grab
a piece of food. Because of the bulk of his clenched fist, he cannot
get his hand through the opening. If he stubbornly persists in
holding on, he will never get his food. If he lets go and figures out
another way to reach his goal, he is more likely to have success.

Sometimes people become stuck in dysfunctional situations be-
cause they are afraid of the unknown. When they become exhausted
from struggling, they may venture out into something new. Many
wonder why they held on for so long. Fear is usually the reason—
fear of lack, fear of harm, fear of failure. Dear ones, I cannot re-
mind you enough that there is nothing to fear! You are supported by
the Universe in all that you do.

Prepare yourself for the journey. Participate in a daily practice
of meditation and exercise. The time for inactivity is over. The
time for movement is now. There is much to do on your mission. I
am with you at all times. You will be guided into right action. Re-
lease attachment to outcomes and be willing to take new paths.
Go forth and be a light to the world. Love to you from your dear
Jahallah.

During the week that I trained to become an angel therapy
practitioner, I attended a shamanic release and renewal ceremony with Dr. Steven Farmer. I have always been drawn to
Native American practices, so I knew this would be a profound experience for me. Each participant was asked to find
an article in nature that attracted us. I chose a piece of lavender

to help me during the ritual. I held it as I focused on the things that were not serving me in my life. I did a meditation with Archangel Michael, and many issues came to the surface. I had a long list of things that I wanted to let go of, but Steven encouraged us to focus on the most important ones.

We were asked to sleep with the article under our pillow or on our nightstand so that it could absorb the energies we released while doing work in our dream state. I asked for assistance in letting go of blocks to my clairvoyance and lack of any kind. I had a clear intention and did a lot of inner work. I think I have a tendency to overdo things at times because I was born on the cusp of Aries and Taurus. In the Native American wheel, my animal totem is the beaver. I had seen a pattern of intense focus and exertion throughout my life. I performed this ritual with my usual intensity. I had eliminated caffeine, red meat, and alcohol in preparation and had done my best to stick to a vegan diet. I knew that something powerful was happening because when I carried the flower to the meeting room the next evening, I could feel pain in my hands. I had to put the lavender in a plastic container because of my discomfort.

There were over 150 people gathered for the ceremony. We were instructed to support each person during this process and the synergy of the group would amplify our efforts. We maintained silence and were smudged with sage before entering the room. We placed our "effigies" on a table until we were ready to release them. We all brought drums and rattles and began a drumming session to build the energy. I immersed myself in the sounds and walked the circle feeling very connected to Mother Earth. When we stopped the first drumming session, I could feel the energy surging through me. A woman next to me broke out in tears because of the powerful sensations.

We can use all of the natural elements to transmute energy, and in past ceremonies I have used water, air, and fire as well as earth. Steven had prepared a large pot of earth to receive our intentions. The use of the earth in this way was very poignant because we were going to plant a tree in it at the end of the ritual. Southern California had been devastated by fires during that week, and it was appropriate that we used this tree to replenish what had been lost. In fact, earlier we all conducted a rain ceremony and were thrilled to see it rain. I took a picture of a rainbow that was shining brilliantly over the ocean the next day.

One by one, people picked up their effigies to place them into the soil. When I went to retrieve my piece of lavender, I could not find it. I spent several minutes looking all around the table, wondering what had happened. I felt myself getting choked up because this ritual was important to me and I had worked so hard to prepare for it. The other participants had begun the next portion of the process and I was standing alone in the back of the room. Self-doubt started to creep in. I know everything that happens in life contains a message. I started to wonder if the universal intelligence thought that my blocks had something more to teach me. I cancelled this negative idea from my mind and tried to figure out what to do next.

My water bottle was at the other end of the room and I was very thirsty. I did not want to disrupt the proceedings by walking through the ceremony, so I took my place in line to release my effigy. We weren't allowed to take personal belongings into the meeting room, but fortunately I had a medicine bag around my neck. One of the stones it contained was a piece of rose quartz. I thought that it would be a fitting gift to release love back into the earth. I held the crystal and infused it with my energy. However, I didn't have much time to analyze all of my life issues and ascertain what was in the most need of healing. I had to quickly focus on what was the most important lesson for me in that moment. My inner voice said, "I let go of the need to control external circumstances. I surrender personal will to Divine will."

I blew those emotions into the stone and dropped it in the pot. I passed by the tree and honored its spirit. I moved to a group of elders and one sprinkled holy water over my head. I returned to my seat and felt much lighter. I could see the value in the way this process had unfolded. I knew that if I did let go and let God guide my life, all would be well. I knew that it was God's perfect design that each one of us should experience abundance. There were no limits that could not be overcome when we became an open channel for Spirit. We ended the ritual with celebration. We drummed and danced around the circle, certain that the future would be brighter.

The next day I performed an angel oracle card reading for a classmate. I have always had the gift of clairsentience, but I still did not see images in my third eye. I gave him the best reading that I could and knew that my sight would be clear in time. I let go of any expectations and continued to practice. On the last day of the retreat, the crowd was applauding each other for doing a great job. I closed my eyes and saw an angel clapping in my mind's eye. I was startled and opened my eyes quickly. I felt angel bumps all over my body, and my eyes filled with tears. I knew that my heavenly helpers appreciated the work that I had done to heal and grow.

Angel of Release Prayer

"Mother-Father God, I am willing to release all things that bring me pain and constriction. I allow Divine flow to move through my life and remove all obstacles to love and peace. As I let go, I open up channels to receive abundance and grace. I will take chances and savor the richness of life. I open myself up to the many wonderful people and experiences that this world has to offer. I relinquish the need to control and let God's will be done. And so it is."

Three ways that I will experience release in my life are . . .

1.

2.

3.

IDEAS:

1. Create a personal ceremony to release old concerns or problems.

2. Buy a bird from a pet store and let it fly free.

3. Call someone who bothers you to say something nice to them.

giving

We make a living by what we get, but we make a
life by what we give.

SIR WINSTON CHURCHILL

*Thank you for this opportunity to share. It is my desire to help
guide you in the way of Light. You are being asked to dedicate an
hour a day to channeling and receiving messages. This will be facilitated by meditation. You put a great effort into bringing light
beings together for holy gatherings. Your work does not go unno-
ticed in the spiritual realms. Bringing people together in a place of
worship is a valuable contribution to society. The energetic shifts
created by these endeavors are of great benefit to the world.*

*Because you are willing to be a channel for Spirit, you will be
supported. You have gained a greater understanding of the dynamic
of giving and receiving during this past year. You have embraced
many opportunities to give without attachment, and you have felt
the lack of constriction and the freedom that this brings. When
people get caught up in the energy of greed and self-preservation, it*

creates a block to the flow of love. Many young souls on the planet are competing for resources to such a degree that they are waging war and causing mass destruction.

If they only knew the universal laws of giving and receiving, they would not be engaged in these self-defeating activities. What you give to another, you give to yourself. We are all one. We are going through a period of remembering this and will return again to rejoin the aspects of the One that now appear separate. Have you ever noticed that when people share, the goodwill is amplified and spreads quickly? Try extending your generosity one step further than you usually do, and notice a lightening of your body and spirit.

Grasping and holding onto things creates a density. It takes more energy to maintain these states than it does to let go. Several times during my last incarnation I was tempted to hold on to material possessions. My existence as a "holy man" was supported by donations and alms. Sometimes I would become hungry and would have to maintain my faith that the Creator would provide my next meal. On one of these occasions, an elderly woman gave me some bread to eat. I felt like devouring the morsel immediately, but gathered my energy together to talk with her and offer spiritual guidance. When she left, I placed the food in front of me and prepared to eat.

At that moment, I heard the cry of a child coming from a nearby alley. I walked over to see what was happening. The child was on her way home from the market and she had dropped her parcel into the mud. The food was ruined and you could tell by the look in her eyes that she was hungry. I wiped away her tears, *gave her my bread, and sent her on her way. As I returned to my camp, I found five visitors waiting for me. They had spread out a picnic luncheon with many savory treats. We enjoyed the abundance together, and I was filled to overflowing.*

The souls who ascend to the higher planes and have no need to reincarnate have given up their attachments. I am not advocating the path of poverty and asceticism, but I would encourage you to let go of the things in your life that are weighing you down. Sometimes people's possessions begin to own them. It takes much effort and responsibility to maintain them. If you conduct periodic "spring cleanings," you will find that the energy in your home will lift. Circulate things that you no longer use. The joy created by those who receive your gifts will return to you.

Sometimes when you are asked to give of yourself, there is resistance. It is a human characteristic to "look out for number one." There is no need to sacrifice your well-being in order to give. There is plenty for you to live comfortably and plenty for you to share with others. Giving is not just something we do with physical objects. When we extend ourselves in love and offer assistance to others, the rewards are great. You can share spiritual truths or special talents. Don't begrudge sharing what you have been given. Appreciate the fact that you have much to offer. Om Shanti, Jahallah.

I coordinated a harp concert and workshop with Peter Sterling and Laura Lee called "Angels Among Us." I spent a lot a time advertising and preparing for the event. I visited every metaphysical gathering place that I could think of and contacted newspapers, radio stations, and universities. For weeks

I was in a state of low-level anxiety because I wanted as many people as possible to experience the healing music and spiritual guidance that this program would create. Laura and Peter were driving from Northern California to be with us, and I hoped the experience would be profitable for everyone.

Many people responded to my e-mails saying that they could not attend due to other commitments. My colleague and I were a bit nervous because we wanted the event to be a success. She was preparing a lovely buffet for our guests and putting a lot of effort into making it a special occasion. During the week before the concert, I suddenly felt a calmness about the situation and trusted that the Universe would create a gathering where everyone's needs were met. I knew that it would be a holy encounter.

This trust coincided with my dedication to channel Jahallah and communicate with the angels. Each day I chose an angelic energy and brought that into my experience. On the day that I chose the Angel of Trust, I understood that God's angels go before me daily to prepare my way. As I lived in the present moment, I could experience peace and joy from trusting in the Divine flow. I asked for the assistance of my angels and guides in attracting people to our gathering.

I had taken a step toward releasing my ego concerns and focusing on the reason we were doing this work. Our purpose was to create a place where all paths to God were honored and where people could find spiritual healing. The workshop turned out to be a lovely gathering, and the energy of Divine presence was strong.

Laura spoke of the angelic realms and her life-changing experiences with the angels. Peter created an altar in the center of the room with crystals, artwork, and sacred geometry. In a guided meditation, we cleared our energies with essential oils, bells, and gongs. We were directed to call in an angel who would give us a gift. The Angel of Joy came to me with a box. When I opened it, I could only sense energy swirling out.

Inwardly, I said, "I don't get it." Instantly, the response was, "The music is the gift." The impact was strong and I remembered all of the times I had played Peter's CD, *The Angel's Gift*, during my healing work. It always created a soothing, healing energy that brought me great joy.

As Peter played the harp, my eyes filled with tears. I knew that all of my efforts to create a spiritual gathering place were being honored. When I was able to give without attachment, I was given priceless gifts from the spiritual realms. It was a blessing to see other members of the group receiving profound insights that night. I know the angels were with the group, reminding us that as we give, we receive.

Angel of Giving Prayer

"Mother-Father God, on this special day I send forth gratitude for the giving that is occurring all over the world. Let us focus on ways to help and heal each other. I give freely of my love and abilities, and I know that this energy will be returned. We live in a reciprocal universe. We can learn much from observing the

way the earth gives freely of itself to sustain and nurture us. Our Creator cares for every living creature
without attachments or expectations. And so it is."

Three ways that I will experience giving in my life are . . .
1.

2.

3.

IDEAS:
1. Buy a Happy Meal and give the toy to a passing child.

2. Donate time to a local homeless shelter.

3. Write out a check to your favorite charity.

gratitude

Gratitude to God becomes the way in which He is
remembered, for love cannot be far behind a grateful heart and thankful mind.

A COURSE IN MIRACLES

*You are moving forward on this journey with eager steps. You are
taking great strides toward recognizing who you truly are as
Spirit. You will begin to notice that as I bring words through, the
sensations of tenderness and acceptance will be present. My goals
are not to control and coerce, but to gently be of service for guidance. I would like to express gratitude for your willingness to be a
channel for this information.*

*Can you remember a time when you were very grateful? What
was the experience like? Did someone else reach out to help you?
If so, make it your intention this week to reach out in a similar
way to someone else. You will be able to spread the joy that you
received. Send praise to your Creator for the many gifts you are
given. Appreciate yourself for the many ways that you share love.*

View yourself as an extension of God and allow yourself to be an instrument of his work. Because you are willing to be of service, even more blessings will return to you.

You will reach many people who will resonate with your manner of sharing truth. Always remember to be authentic with yourself and others. There is shadow and light present in each human experience. Scrutinize your inner world and shine the light into all the dark places. You will feel a greater peace, joy, and lightness in your life as you release what no longer serves your highest good.

Surround yourself with high-minded, loving individuals who will bolster your light and help amplify its radiance. Surrendering to Divine will is a key factor in graduating from one level of consciousness to another. Release of your ego self will allow greater power and energy to move through your vehicle, transporting you to higher realms. Be grateful for the many ways the blessings of your Creator are manifesting in your life. Gratitude attracts more blessings. All things of creation are cyclical.

When I was young, I had the opportunity to visit my cousins in a city far to the east. I was going to travel by myself for the first time. I had a donkey to carry my belongings. I was excited about this new adventure. When I entered the city walls, I saw a goat. It looked lost, so I tied a rope around its neck and led it through the town.

I met with my cousins and they said that the goat did not look familiar. We gave it some food and water and went to sleep. In the morning, a large crowd of people gathered outside. They asked for the goat. When I brought the animal to them, they declared that it belonged to the emperor. It had a brand with the ruler's symbol. A *young boy came through the crowd and wrapped his arms lovingly around the goat's neck. He had been responsible for the care of the animal and had lost track of it. The boy was extremely grateful that his charge had been returned and that he would be safe from punishment. He gave me his blessing and joyfully led the animal back home.*

This story reminds us that we sometimes lose our way, but when we return, the joy and gratitude are magnified. I would ask each of you to go within now and take into account all of the blessings in your life. Can you even be grateful for the situations you would deem "learning experiences" or "challenges"? Try to find one glimmer of benefit in each aspect of your life, and you will uplift your energy field. If you fall short, be assured that the place of peace where your true self resides does not waver in its love and acceptance. You will always find your way home.

Have you ever wondered what would happen if all the people in the world were grateful at the same time? It would create an extremely powerful and vibrant energy field. Gratitude is a dynamic energy that can uplift and transform. Take advantage of this simple tool for evolution and expansion. We are grateful for these opportunities to share and grow with you. Good tidings, Jahallah.

On the morning that I planned to write this chapter, I was on the Internet answering my e-mails and visiting a few Web sites. I love to read my daily *Cathy* comics, and sometimes I go to the Voyager Tarot site and pick a card for the day. On this occasion, the card that came up was the "Woman of Cups—The Rejoicer." I thought that was really appropriate for the energy I was in. The card depicted three women enjoying the elements of nature. Two had water cascading over them. Lotus flowers and water lilies were prominent in the picture.

The card was significant to me because I am in the moment and steeped in gratitude when I am in the water. My e-mail address is "AWaterlily444" because of this dynamic. The flowers are symbolic to me of finding inner stillness and greater spiritual depths. The "444" indicates that the angels are active in my life.

I went about my morning routine and thought about the many reasons I had to be grateful. I can honestly say that at forty years of age, I was enjoying my life more than I ever had before. My children were all in high school and I really appreciated it when they helped out with household chores. They usually did well in school, and I was very proud of them. My husband worked hard at his job every day and enjoyed spending time with the family.

My mornings were quiet and I had time to write my books and network on the computer for my employer and my Web site practitioners. I would do housework and swim in the pool. One of the highlights of each day was the moment that I dove into the sparkling water. (Granted, I spent more time cleaning the pool than I did swimming in it, but it was worth it.) Every day I thanked the Universe for all the beauty I was experiencing. Some days, I was so happy that I would laugh out loud.

I immersed myself in the sunshine and water, enjoying the company of birds, butterflies, and my English bulldog, Toots.

In the afternoons, I went to work. I met wonderful people in a beautiful, Spirit-filled environment. It was great being able to wear comfortable "hippie clothes" and go barefoot. My employer was cheerful, easygoing, and generous. We enjoyed putting on programs, and on many evenings I attended classes and workshops for my own personal growth. I also performed healing sessions during my free time.

I am very grateful to have positive people in my life. I grew up in a household that made connection with God a priority. My parents, Don and Joyce, have always been supportive and encouraged me to follow my heart. My brother, Jonathan, is always available to provide motivation and a good laugh. It is important to surround yourself with like-minded people who are dedicated to spiritual growth. My friends and I have a lot of fun exploring new things in the world of metaphysics.

During the years that I spent working in this field, I learned some wonderful lessons. I became certain that we are powerful cocreators with God and that we can manifest the life of our dreams by applying spiritual principles. I discovered the benefits of being grateful. It uplifts your spirits and attracts more good things to appreciate. One year I kept a "gratitude journal." Every evening I would list the things that I appreciated during the day. Granted, on some occasions I made entries such as "I survived," but for the most part it was a great tool for focusing on the good in my life.

I usually don't keep many mementos, but I kept my journal because it is fun to read occasionally when I need a boost. One entry said, "Sunday, November 22, 1998—Larry took me out for dinner and I ate spring rolls with raspberry sauce at Wolfgang Puck's restaurant. Anthony told me that I was a special person. Things I appreciate: white roses, Zion National Park, writers of inspirational books, water, romantic comedies, *A Course in Miracles*, fruit trees, sleep."

My mother hung a sign in her kitchen that read, "Normal day—let me be aware of the treasure you are." That was a good reminder to take a look around and embrace each beautiful moment. I live a pretty simple life, but I like it. I know it will continue to change in a continuous ebb and flow. I think we have truly mastered gratitude when we can appreciate even the difficulties in our lives. I had one rough day, but I wrote in my gratitude journal, "I am glad that I will manifest a car that does not stall in intersections and that has a functioning air conditioner." I am happy to say that this goal has been accomplished, and I know that things will continue to improve as I extend gratitude for what I have now.

Angel of Gratitude Prayer

"Mother-Father God, I give thanks and praise for the many ways in which I am blessed. My life is filled with people and experiences that bring me joy. I am grateful for the wonders of nature and the creativity of mankind. I acknowledge the beauty within myself. I am a powerful being of light with unlimited potential to manifest great things. Even though there have been times when I have lost my way, I am grateful to be in the Divine flow of life as an irreplaceable part of the One. And so it is."

Three ways that I will experience gratitude in my life are . . .
1.

2.

3.

IDEAS:

1. Start a gratitude journal.

2. Call a friend and thank them for the good times you share.

3. Say thank-you thirty-three times in one day (to God, yourself, and others).

belief

All we are is the result of what we have thought.
The mind is everything. What we think, we
become.

BUDDHA

*Because I am speaking to you about belief, you must believe that
this message will be clear. Many times in the past my message
has been blocked because you did not believe in yourself. Spirit
communication is good practice for developing trust and belief in
spiritual guidance. You are embarking on a journey that will lead
you to the "promised land." This is not a far-off destination. It is
as close as a thought, a belief, a choice.*

*Elementary school students study geography. They are taught
how to locate places on a map. I would like to teach you to locate
a very holy place. It is the place where your higher self resides. It
is within your heart. Beliefs are created with the mind, and truth
is found in your heart. Remember to go within and you will find
enlightenment.*

Begin by investing a few moments each day believing that you are loved. Experience what it feels like to be loved. Enjoy the sensations running through your physical body. Notice that constriction is released and you become even more open to receive. You are loved at every moment. Sometimes you forget. I am here to remind you that there are no limits to the love that is available to you. Experience the healing power of God's love at any time. Wash away the old hurts and embrace a new beginning today. Before time began, there was only the inner prompting of Spirit that motivated movement. That prompting was love, which extended itself and generated more.

Do you believe the things that I say? The world was created from the Loving Word. Emotions, words, and beliefs shape reality. Watch your words carefully because they have much power to create. When you believe that circumstances are beyond your control, you are not accessing all of the power within you to produce change. Sometimes you try to focus on a desired outcome and then lose interest. Sometimes you don't really believe that you can have the abundance that awaits you. It is time to release ambiguity!

When you lose focus or change your mind, your energy moves elsewhere. This is common, but I would encourage you not to become ambiguous about doing your spiritual work. It is the force that will give energy and power to all of your endeavors. Transformation takes place when we open ourselves to hear the voice of God. When you are willing to listen, your way will be made easy.

When I was a child on the earth, I was gathering vegetables from the garden one day. I found a large tomato with a fat worm in it. I was disgusted and threw the tomato across the field. My fa-

ther came by and picked it up. "Listen, son," he said, "This tomato should not be wasted. We can mix it into the pig's food. It is a gift from the Creator and it is right that it should be shared."

I wondered how any creature would want to eat that spoiled tomato. I had a belief that it wasn't good enough. Later I watched a pig savor the morsel with his meal. I reconsidered my belief in its value. I felt love as I watched the animal receive the sustenance that he needed. I realized that we cannot always accurately judge what is of worth and what is not. It is only our beliefs that make something real for us.

Believe that you have valuable gifts to share. There will be many who will need to hear your ideas expressed. Just as you are uplifted and encouraged today, others will receive a tasty morsel from each of your words. Life is like a banquet with different tastes to choose from. People will find the spiritual food that is right for them.

We have many beliefs that are passed down to us from generation to generation. You might stop to ask yourself where they originated and why you hold on to them. Do you believe something just because an "authority figure" told you it was true? Or did you accept the belief because of your own firsthand experience? I love the exploration of metaphysics because it is all about stretching yourself—your perceptions, your abilities, and your beliefs. It is all about understanding the universe through personal exploration.

I admit that when I first approached "those books" on the shelf at the library, my Southern Baptist sensibilities were threatened. I had beliefs that were generated by fear-based thinking, and I needed to move beyond them. I had been taught that the paranormal would lead you down the path of destruction. However, I braced myself and started to read anyway. What I found instead was a path toward enlightenment. I read everything that I could get my hands on. The subjects ranged from alien visitation to near-death experiences. I read about spirit communication, astral projection, and meditation. I studied spiritual paths from indigenous cultures and ancient mystics.

I took what I needed from each philosophy and left the rest behind. I formulated my own belief system based on what resonated with my higher guidance. It was such a relief to release judgments about other religions and embrace the common ideas that we all share. I learned how significantly our belief systems shape our lives. Wayne Dyer wrote a book called *You'll See It When You Believe It.* That book contained a powerful lesson that gave me a greater understanding of how we create our own realities.

I think that our biggest challenge is believing in ourselves. We all have God-given abilities, but in order to access them we need to move beyond our limited perceptions. We are all "wired up" to be psychics and healers, and it is up to us to be receptive to those gifts. It took me about two years of performing hands-on healings before I believed that I was being truly effective. Even though gifted psychic counselors had given me a lot of validation, I needed to accept and acknowledge myself. I admit that there were a few people in my life who scoffed at the work I did, but they were the ones who had an unwillingness to explore it for themselves.

I remember the day I totally let go of my self-imposed beliefs in limitation. I received a call from a woman who had seen my Web site and wanted to experience a healing from the emotional and mental stresses she was experiencing. Instead of being caught up in performance anxiety, my main focus was becoming an instrument for Spirit. I began the session with an oracle card reading that was very uplifting. The words came easily, and I was inspired to share various tools that had helped me on my journey. Throughout the session, I followed my intuition and was immersed in the flow. I employed various techniques and concluded with a Christ Force healing that left me tingling and filled with joy. I continued my work with renewed enthusiasm and left doubt behind.

It is easy to believe when we have peak experiences or "aha" moments. The real accomplishment is maintaining our faith during everyday challenges. It is imperative that we believe in the inherent goodness of the Universe despite outward appearances. The truth of that belief will come shining through even in the darkest times. Beliefs can change as we explore, evolve, and increase our awareness. However, the love that our Creator has for us is the one thing that does not change.

Angel of Belief Prayer

"Mother-Father God, I believe that I dwell in a world
that is safe and filled with abundance. I have the power
within me to create the life of my dreams. I have loving
people and spirit guides that nurture and support me.
I see the value in all of my experiences and find the
lessons that help me to evolve. I am strengthening my
connection with my Creator. I believe that I can access
and use my spiritual gifts to heal myself and others.
And so it is."

Three ways that I experience belief in my life are . . .

1.

2.

3.

IDEAS:

1. Hold something that you don't like and reconsider your
   belief about it.

2. Make a list of five positive beliefs you hold about the
   world.

3. Believe in yourself and engage in an activity that you
   didn't think you could do well.

peace

*Peace be with you, now and always. This is one of the most power-
ful blessings that I can give you. Peace is a gift that is immeasur-
able in its value. It is a goal that many seek and few achieve. Why
is this? Perhaps it is due to the ever-increasing need for stimulus in
your society. People are constantly seeking more activity in an effort to gain fulfillment. They seek something outside of themselves
for comfort. This cycle will be perpetual because peace can only be
achieved by releasing attachment to external circumstances.*

*We were created in a state of peace, and it can be accessed by
going within and remembering it. Feel the marvelous sensation it
brings as you allow yourself to be supported by the Creator. There
is no need for you to fret, worry, or be agitated. You are being cared
for by an unseen Power. Peace is your birthright, and you always
have the ability to choose peace instead of turmoil.*

Wars have been waged because of inner dissatisfaction. This unrest is projected outward and dissension takes place. Can peace possibly be gained by acts of violence? Of course not. Temporary submission may occur, but the inner feelings of anger and rage will remain until they erupt again. We are working diligently on the spiritual planes to help people create peace on earth. As each person realizes inner peace, it will affect the entire planet. "Fighting against" war and violence will only lend energy to them. Remove your energy from feeding this dynamic and it will eventually cease.

Many of you have not chosen war as a part of your experience. You can view it from the safety of your living rooms, and it has very little effect on your lives. Basically, all it has done is to incite emotions. Some are outraged and angry. Some are compassionate and motivated to extend themselves to be of assistance. Many have understood that their inner work will have a great impact on creating a peace consciousness, and they have been working diligently to raise awareness. Peace incites passion and commitment in those who understand its value.

When I was on earth, I was walking through a field to get to the main road. I saw a band of men in a confrontation with a farmer. He told them to leave his property or else he would resort to violent measures. At first they were willing to leave, but the farmer's antagonism incited their anger. They became indignant and said, "Who does this man think he is, fencing off the land to withhold it from others?"

They were doing no harm and should have had the right to peacefully pass through. The men started to fight, and a few were *left with cuts and bruises. The farmer freed himself from the melee and came back brandishing a huge machete. The men ran for shelter and found some rocks to throw. The battle finally died down, and the men went on their way. I was a bit nervous, not knowing how I was going to reach the main road without crossing the farmer's property. I started to cautiously make my way when I heard a shout. He saw me and signaled for me to come over.*

"What are you doing here?" he demanded. I told him that I was just passing through and did not want any trouble. He didn't seem threatened by me. It seemed like he wanted to talk. He told me that he had been worried about the safety of his family since marauders had come and ransacked his home. He thought that the men he had fought with were up to no good. "How will I ever feel safe again?" he asked.

I told him that when I felt afraid, I would go within to find the Source of peace. I didn't believe any harm would come to me if I was in alignment with Divine will. That enabled me to maintain peace with myself and others. He was desperately seeking release from the turmoil in his life. He found out firsthand that violence only begets more violence. I think he may have considered my advice. We parted ways with a wave good-bye.

In truth, there is nothing to be feared and nothing to be lost. Much strife and competition would be eliminated if people understood this. We have everything we need at our disposal. There are solutions to all of the world's problems if people would join together to solve them. Be certain that as you create harmony within yourself and find peaceful solutions to your own problems, it will add to raising the consciousness of the planet. Please dedicate yourself fully to this task. You will be greatly rewarded when you do. Peace and blessings, Jahallah.

On the morning of 9/11, a switch turned on inside of me, and my life changed. An inner voice said, "It's time to get to work." I had been a student of metaphysics and world religions for many years. I spent a lot of time reading books but didn't put much of the information into application. I then received loud reminders about my soul's purpose and the necessity for moving into action. I left my job and dedicated myself to healing work, counseling and coordinating programs for spiritual organizations.

In a past-life reading, a psychic told me that in a previous incarnation I lived in the Middle East. I created a gathering place where people of different religions and cultures could join together peacefully and exchange information. That sounded like a fabulous experience, but I didn't see how it applied to my life. Several years later I found myself developing the Spiritual Awareness Network to produce a similar dynamic.

I feel strongly that as we gain understanding and acceptance of the diversity of the human condition, we will help to heal the mass consciousness and establish peace on earth. I was inspired by an e-mail I received discussing how each of us has the power, through our thoughts and emotions, to influence the energy of the planet. People must use their thoughts wisely and understand their power. It is a universal law that thoughts become their physical equivalent.

To create peace in your external world, focus on creating peace within yourself. Whatever you give your attention to increases. Change your thoughts of anger, hatred, retribution, and fear to those of peace, compassion, tolerance, and love. I avoid watching the news because it can keep people afraid and disempowered. I encourage you to go within for your guidance. As you develop wholeness in your personal life, it will be reflected outwardly to help the global consciousness.

Ask your angels, guides, and ascended masters to protect and uplift you. Remember, however, that they can only do their work in an atmosphere of compassion, not condemnation. Keep your thoughts and actions focused on the positive and you will be able to manifest great things.

On the third anniversary of 9/11, I decided to celebrate my "re-birthday" in a way that would add to the global peace consciousness. I organized a peace awareness festival at an alternative health institute near my home. We offered services such as aura imaging, tarot reading, mediumship, healing, massage, homeopathy, and reflexology. Each practitioner was asked to use their services and lectures in a way that would promote and teach peace. No matter what we do in life, we can bring peace into our interactions with others.

My friend Deanna Joseph demonstrated this by singing beautiful, peaceful songs, such as John Lennon's "Imagine." A talented artist named Betsey Webster created an original piece of sidewalk art in front of the festival. She drew a lovely goddess-type figure embracing a globe. A homeless man pushing a shopping cart stopped in front of the picture and smiled.

Betsey and I smiled as well, knowing that our message had been received.

Each of us has chosen to incarnate at this time for a special reason. Our actions will be a great catalyst for putting an end to warfare and creating peace in our world. It is no accident that you are reading this information now. You are a lightworker and a peacemaker. It is time to get to work.

Angel of Peace Prayer

"Mother–Father God, I pray to experience the peace that surpasses all understanding. I am willing to release any fear or unforgiveness that would block my connection with You. As I connect with this energy, I can be assured that all is well. I am always free to choose peace instead of conflict. I am rededicating myself to extend this energy to others. I am here to be a spiritual peacemaker and I embrace my role. I am at peace now. And so it is."

Three ways that I will experience peace in my life are . . .

1.

2.

3.

IDEAS:

1. Attend a peace rally with like-minded people.

2. Do a guided meditation and prayer to surround the world with peaceful energy.

3. Create a piece of artwork with a peace-related theme and share it with others.

patience

> Patience is power; with time and patience, the
> mulberry leaf becomes silk.
>
> CHINESE PROVERB

Patience brings you peace of mind. There is nothing you can do to speed up the process of life. Everything happens according to Divine timing. All the worry and stress in the world are not going to change external circumstances. Actually, they might seem to prolong the situations with which you are not at peace. Every time you are tempted to be impatient, it is a reminder to go within and access your Source of peace.

Watch the rhythms of nature and see them unfolding according to an ingenious pattern. You cannot speed the process of flowers blooming or butterflies emerging. If you tried, you would damage the creation. Humans have a great aversion to waiting for things. They have developed a "microwave mentality," wanting everything to be instantaneous. Instant gratification is not always the best way to experience growth. In fact, it tends to make people more dependent on having their needs met instantly. Years ago, you didn't worry too much about having to change a television station yourself or having to wait for a slow computer. Now it seems intolerable since your capacity for waiting has been diminished.

On the other side, things do manifest quickly according to your thoughts and desires. The earth is a training ground that allows you to take your time in creating so that you have a clearer vision of what it is that you really want. In this manner, you will be able to see the consequences of those choices. Waiting eliminates trauma at times. Think of situations in which you acted out of anger and wanted something bad to happen to another out of retribution. If that had manifested quickly, a downward spiral of events would have been triggered.

Patience and perfect timing are actually attributes designed for your own protection and evolution. Can you remember a time when you really wanted something and had a strong attachment to getting it? The goal seemed to remain just out of reach until you surrendered the "need" for it. Also, you may have experienced times when you wanted something and later found out it would not have been in your best interests. The waiting period and your patience allowed something better to come into your life, and you were glad that you did not get the original desire.

When I was on the earth plane, there were many opportunities to practice patience. Since we lived in an agricultural community, you quickly learned that the cycles of nature could not be rushed. There was a time for planting, a time for nurturing, and a time for harvest. We needed to work hard when it was time for each task and followed it through to completion. My favorite memories were *of the times we enjoyed the benefits of our labors. I loved to help my grandmother preserve food for the winter. When our work was complete, we would celebrate by eating a great feast.*

You have been told, "Patience is a virtue." What is a virtue? It is a quality that benefits you and others. It causes no harm. It is power associated with strength, purity, and worth. It is something intrinsically valuable. In the future, instead of resisting a lesson in patience, welcome the opportunity to bring this beneficial quality into your life. Practicing patience is a gift that you are giving yourself. Being impatient only causes stress on your mind, body, and emotions. You are only harming yourself by becoming aggravated, so treat yourself kindly and don't resist what is happening.

Spirit communication has been an exercise in patience for you. On some days you felt blocked and wanted immediate results. You found that when you released attachment to the outcome and did your best, the flow was restarted. Meditation causes some people similar frustration. The purpose of the meditation is totally defeated when you are impatient. The Buddha practiced nonresistance and surrender. Don't misinterpret the word surrender. It does not mean that you should not take Spirit-directed action in your life. It just means that you can keep your mind in a state of peace and acceptance. Pretend that you are in a situation where you are growing impatient. How does that feel? What sensations are you feeling on an emotional and physical level? It probably is not pleasant. Now pretend that you are not hurrying or forcing or worrying. Doesn't this peaceful sensation make your body and mind feel balanced and in harmony?

In your country, there are many opportunities to wait in lines. Rejoice that you are being given these chances to practice patience until it becomes effortless. The next time you are in line and it is moving slowly, stop to be aware of the present moment. Think of its sacredness and of your connection to the people around you. If anyone is becoming anxious or aggravated, you may notice the energy spreading to others. Try to send the gathering unconditional love and peace. You may see a shift take place immediately. You are here to be a lightworker because you have a remembrance of who you truly are. It is your job to remind others of their birthright. Since we are all connected, what you do for another, you are doing for yourself. As one person makes a shift, it makes an impact on all of humanity.

If you are having trouble with this, you can always ask your angels and guides for assistance. They can help you change your vibratory frequency. You can feel the energetic change take place within you. The energy of patience creates peace. Impatience blocks your awareness of the value in the present moment. If you are truly "practicing the presence," impatience will not exist. Don't forget that the "present" is a "gift." Open it and experience the joy. Your beloved, Jahallah.

I remember a time when I really needed to practice patience so that my highest good would be served. Housing is a very important issue for most people. When my husband and I got married, we had a sweet little home in Whittier, California. We lived there happily after our first son was born. When the twins came along, we needed more room. All we could afford was a duplex near the freeway in a neighboring suburb. It featured green shag carpet and roaches that crawled on you while you were sleeping.

We stayed there for a year or so, but I could not stand it any longer. I "knew" that I was moving, but I did not know where. We received a telephone call from a relative telling us that a rental home in Riverside had just opened up. It was a four-bedroom house on a huge lot for less than we were paying for our roach motel. We moved and enjoyed several years in that location. When the owner decided to sell the property, I was devastated. Actually, people thought I was overreacting to the problem, but maybe something within me knew what was ahead.

We moved our family of five into a two-bedroom apartment. It was one of the most difficult times of my life. We were crowded, and the apartments were noisy. My husband was like a man lost at sea without his garage and tools. I was working in an unpleasant night job and suffering from depression. I think it was a transformational time for me spiritually. I could not watch any type of violence on television because I was ultrasensitive. I had trouble sleeping and I would lie awake crying. One night I lay on the bed feeling totally separated from God. I prayed fervently for a sign that I would be reconnected and released from my sadness. On another night I got up to get my son some cough medicine, and I felt a presence come through the window. I felt a piercing pain at the back of my heart and fell to my knees.

That really scared me, so I discussed it with a couple of people. Some thought it was spiritual warfare, some thought it was a clearing of the heart chakra. I dedicated myself to finding my own answers. I read New Thought teachings that helped me to shift my worldview. I became more at peace with myself and was stronger in the face of challenges. Eventually, I regained my equilibrium and the extreme sensitivity diminished.

Some nights I would feel tingling sensations throughout my body, and I could feel a Divine presence with me. Sometimes these joyful feelings and tears would keep me up all night as well. Needless to say, I didn't sleep much during this time, and I could hardly wait to find a house. Our intention was to save money for a down payment, but we never seemed to get ahead.

I looked into HUD housing and found a new two-story home in our old neighborhood. It was gorgeous, and I was excited at the prospect of buying it. I showed a picture of it to a psychic friend, and she said that I shouldn't be attached to that specific location. She said that it was lovely, but it would eventually tap us out financially. She said that the Universe would direct us to the best house for our needs.

One morning, I drove two of my children to school, and the third stayed with me because he was running a fever. I decided to take him to mass at a Catholic church and pray for a healing. That was something I didn't usually do, but I had an inner prompting to take that course of action. As we drove to the church, I saw a "for sale" sign in front of a white and green house with a big bay window. It was in an older part of town and had a lot of trees and plants around it.

I peeked inside and everything was newly painted and carpeted. We went around to the back and saw a swimming pool and fruit trees in a large yard. I thought that something so nice would probably be out of our price range, but I called the realtor. He had purchased the home in a foreclosure and was the owner. He gave me the price for the property, which seemed very reasonable. I thanked him for the information, but since I didn't have a down payment I didn't pursue it.

He called back a day later and said that he would help us with the money. We wouldn't have to pay any realtor fees and could just move in! As we sat in his office signing papers, the phone kept ringing with people interested in the property. He had other offers but was determined to help us out. Our mortgage payments were about the same as we were paying for rent at the apartment complex. Even though I lost my job right when the escrow was being processed, everything fell smoothly into place.

I had some time off to enjoy my new home. I loved the swimming pool and Jacuzzi and the spacious yard filled with plums, apricots, oranges, peaches, and nectarines. The first thing I did was to buy a statue of Mary. I put it by the Santa Rosa plum tree. I went outside the next week and found the tree filled with beautiful white blossoms. This symbolized our new beginning, and I was grateful for the miracle that had led us to this place. After that experience, I was convinced that God had a better plan in mind for me than I had for myself.

Since then I have saved myself a great deal of worry, knowing that if I am patient, things will always work out for the best.

Angel of Patience Prayer

"Mother-Father God, I am willing to accept the present moment and see its value. I will savor all of the beauty that surrounds me, even if it seems to be concealed. I have patience, knowing that all the things that I desire will manifest at the perfect time. I do not need to hurry or worry, because everything in my life is happening according to Divine Will. I am in a state of peace, knowing that my Creator is assisting me in all of my endeavors. And so it is."

Three ways that I will experience patience in my life are . . .
1.

2.

3.

IDEAS:
1. Plant a small flower garden.

2. Avoid impulse shopping for one week and then buy with consciousness.

3. Review your life and think of an incident when you benefited from waiting.

celebration

> People are just about as happy as they make up
> their minds to be.
>
> ABRAHAM LINCOLN

*It is most gratifying to have yet another opportunity to share light.
Let us begin by talking about celebration and ceremony. Each day
offers sacred moments to connect with Spirit when you pause to
remember your true self. You have seen how much enthusiasm
and planning goes into traditional holidays. These are times when
people remember to celebrate life. Sometimes these types of rituals
become too commonplace, and their original meanings are lost.*

*I would encourage you to create your own ceremonies to cele-
brate your connection to the Divine. For example, you may want
to dedicate a day to exploring power or joy or abundance or magic.
Many tools can be found at spiritual marketplaces, such as candles, incense, oils, artwork, clothing, and elements of nature. Remember that the tools you use are just symbols to create a connection with that which it represents.*

You may want to write a poem or prayer to say in your ceremony. You could prepare a special food dish that has personal significance to you. You might be inspired to show gratitude for the blessings in your life. I would suggest having thanksgiving celebrations several times a month! You know that blessings continue to flow as you give thanks for them. You can also have a "thanksgetting" day to honor your contributions to life and treat yourself with a special gift.

Another idea might be to designate a special time for releasing. In this manner, you can let go of blocks to abundance, health, and joy. The tools in your ritual might be designed to cleanse your energy field so that you create an empty vessel to fill up with light and love. You could use smudge and even bathe, fast, or cleanse beforehand. Any action you take with a positive, focused intent becomes sacred.

Many people find themselves caught up in routines and rarely have time to do anything different. If you create your own "holy days," you will have many opportunities to experience life from new perspectives. Whenever you are tempted to complain or feel downtrodden, declare a new holiday and celebrate!

You could plan days to commune with nature. You might also want to attend a new spiritual gathering. It is always interesting to visit a temple, mosque, powwow, or other place of worship that you have never been before. If you go with an attitude of acceptance and honor the oneness of all people, I am sure you will gain new understandings that would be an asset to your personal spiritual practice.

There are so many colors in the fabric of life! When we combine all of them, they create a beautiful tapestry. Don't settle for sackcloth when the world is offering you the finest silks. There are treasures everywhere to enhance your journey. Transmute the lead into gold with the alchemy of Spirit. Celebrate the gift of life and share it with others.

I will never forget a wedding feast that I attended when I was a child. I was in awe of the pageantry, music, and sumptuous foods. Everyone dressed in their finest robes and sang and danced into the night. Torches illuminated the gathering and everything sparkled with life. The next day seemed so quiet and ordinary in comparison, so the neighborhood children staged a celebration of their own with the leftover ornaments and food. We had a wonderful time creating music with sticks and rattles and drums. We were reveling in the sacredness of the present moment.

Go out today and do something with enthusiasm and excitement. Many amazing experiences will be revealed to you. Have you ever wondered what would happen if you just released your limitations and acted with total abandon? Wouldn't it be fun to dance with colorful scarves or to make music with a tambourine? Do you think people would judge you? They would probably wish that they were free of their own inhibitions and could revel in the fun of the moment. Dance and sing and play to your heart's content. You are not marching to the tune of a funeral dirge, but to the life-giving heartbeat of the Universe. Celebrate! Jahallah.

I took Jahallah's advice the day we wrote this chapter. I played Celtic music and danced with scarves and instruments. I admit that I hoped my neighbors were not watching through the windows, but I had fun. I performed a ritual with candles, incense, oils, and stones to express thanks for the many blessings in my life. It reminded me of the day we had a fairy circle at a spiritual center. The adults danced around as the children giggled in amusement.

Another celebration I enjoyed was my fortieth birthday party. The theme of the evening was creating peace, and a talented musician friend offered to provide entertainment. She sang inspirational songs and played her keyboard. She asked everyone in attendance to tell me how I had blessed their lives. I tried to hold back the tears as people shared kind words with me. That was a special evening when we celebrated life. It gave me confirmation that I was where I was meant to be.

I am drawn to traditions that honor the earth in celebration. I attended a Beltane gathering one spring. It was another opportunity to let go and play. We made flower garlands for our hair and danced the maypole. We honored the season of spring and the energies of the earth.

During my healing sessions, I use a ritual based on Native practices to create a vortex and call in the elements. Since ritual is a way to bring energy from the spiritual realm into physical manifestation, I feel that this is an effective healing tool. In this empowerment circle ritual, I also call in all aspects of the Creator to bring in universal life-force energy and create a sacred space. I amplify the vortex by placing quartz crystals at each of the four directions. Candles by each crystal enhance the quality of the experience.

In my ritual, the east represents the realm of Spirit, the element of fire, the season of spring, and the human kingdom. The south represents the realm of the emotions, the element of water, the season of summer, and the plant kingdom. The west represents the realm of the body, the element of earth, the season of fall, and the mineral kingdom. The north represents the realm of the mind, the element of air, the season of winter, and the animal kingdom.

I also invoke the Spirit of the Heavens or Grandfather Sky. It is a masculine, empowering force. Then I invoke the Spirit of Nature or Grandmother Earth. It is a feminine, nurturing force. I ask my spirit helpers to clear all negative energy from my sacred healing circle. I use drumming and the ringing of chimes to raise the vibrations. In my healing work I like to have fun, be creative, and feel the Divine within me being expressed into the physical world.

I encourage people to be creative and celebrate the sacredness in each day. Sometimes we get caught up in routines and work and we forget to play. I always find that going on an outing to the mountains or the beach helps me to be in the moment and acknowledge the beauty that is all around me. After I finish writing this, I am going to take the afternoon off and celebrate!

Angel of Celebration Prayer

"Mother-Father God, I honor and acknowledge You
as the Source of all good. Every day holds within it a
cause for celebration. I will rededicate myself to experience this with joy and creativity. I live in an abundant world and all is perfect in my universe. I honor
the gifts of the earth and acknowledge their sacredness. I appreciate my blessings and give thanks to
God. I celebrate the miracles of my life in every moment. And so it is."

Three ways that I will experience celebration in my life are . . .

1.

2.

3.

IDEAS:

1. Create your own unique holiday and have a special
   meal with close friends.

2. Dance in the forest.

3. Send someone a special gift in the mail celebrating their
   presence in your life.

clarity

What we see in the outer is but a reflection of the inner, because we surround ourselves with a picture of our own beliefs.

EMMET FOX

Clarity comes to us when we focus on what it is we want. Send out clear messages to the Universe, because it responds to your intent. One way to do this is to use affirmations. Energize them with your beliefs and positive emotions. Use all of your senses to visualize and feel what your dreams would be like as reality. What would it taste, feel, sound, smell, and look like?

If you believe yourself to be a victim, the Universe will respond to the signals you are sending out. It is a system of like attracting like. If you are constantly affirming that you are in lack, that message will be received. Being in the moment will help you to manifest. The present moment does not have energies of the past or present confusing it. Experience yourself with wealth, health, love, and joy, and it will be so. Go within and feel those sensations now. They are your reality.

Use your breath as a tool that brings you into focus. Use it to flush your energy field and release any blocks and clogged energy. Spirit communication creates an avenue for information to come in. Right now, I would like you to create an energy channel or opening designed to accept the love and light that are all around you.

Creating simplicity is a means for gaining clarity. When you simplify and remove excess clutter, all that is valuable in your life remains. Examine your daily activities and see which activities are useful to you and which are actually burdens. When you excavate the unnecessary possessions and actions, you will find your authentic self. Who you are and what you want out of life become clearer. Once you uncover those things, make a commitment to bring those qualities into your experience.

Perhaps you have imagined that a particular thing or event was going to bring you fulfillment. When you actually accomplished the goal, it left you feeling empty. If that ever happens in the future, remind yourself that the void within you needs to be filled by Spirit. If the physical world seems unsupportive, remember your network of friends in the heavenly realms. They are as real and active in your life as anyone in the third-dimensional reality. They are in the realm of pure light and goodness. Belief is not required to tap into this source of energy. It exists all around you every day.

Have you ever been in a dream and you sense something before you, yet your vision is obscured? It is the same in your waking dream. The light is present, yet you may have difficulty seeing it. In the book of Genesis, a story is told of the creation of All That Is. God said, "Let there be light," and it was so. You can use your word and intention to bring light to your life. There is no way that this cannot be so if your intention is strong.

Sometimes humans vacillate between wanting the light and wanting to hold strong to the illusion. The ego self finds comfort in "being right" or "being in control." As soon as you release these needs, the light will come pouring through. All unforgiveness and fear will be cleared away, and all that will be left is the clarity of your purpose and the purity of your true essence.

There was an old, blind man in our village who people went to for counsel. Even though he didn't have the use of his eyes, he used his inner sight to gain information. He could "see through" the illusions in people's lives and help them find the truth. Once I asked him if I would ever accomplish great things, and he told me that by breathing in and breathing out I was doing remarkably well. He didn't take life too seriously, and he was an invaluable role model for me.

The only requirements for receiving the abundance of the universe are for you to become clear about what you want and open yourself up to receive it. You can also extend your gifts to others so that the cycle will continue. Let the fog of confusion be lifted now so that you use God's vision to see the blessings your life can contain. With clarity and light, Jahallah.

I remember a time in my life when it seemed like I was covered in a heavy cloud. I was working for a government agency that had a reputation for creating disgruntled employees. The environment was rather toxic, and we worked under stressful conditions. A few weeks after I started the job, a notice went up on the wall asking, "Are you suffering from these signs of depression?" It seemed that I had quite a few of the symptoms. Apparently they had come across this problem before and had established a hotline for people to seek help.

For many months, I would sit at my computer terminal surrounded by hundreds of other unhappy people and feel totally overwhelmed. We couldn't speak and had our bathroom breaks timed. We were being randomly tested for speed and accuracy at all times. We would be forced to work late without notice or we would be written up as AWOL. I think that because I am so sensitive, I was also picking up on the despair of those around me. Tears would stream down my face, but no one noticed because they had quotas to meet.

I went to an HMO psychiatrist who was extremely ineffective as a counselor. He prescribed medication and I took it for a couple of days. I could not tolerate the feeling it created within me, so I stopped taking it. I had to find another way out of the fog. One method might have been for me to leave the job, but I needed the money. Fortunately, the work was so repetitive that I was able to listen to books on tape as I typed on the computer. I managed to get quite an education in metaphysics and spiritual growth. One book in particular really helped me out. It was called *Messages to Our Family* by Byron and Annie Kirkwood.

It consisted of channeled information from Jesus, Mother Mary, and the Great White Brotherhood. It is one of the few books I have read more than once. I even taped myself reading certain passages and listened to them when I needed a boost.

One day I was listening to my tape, and the fog just lifted. The clarity and relief I experienced were unforgettable. I cried tears of joy instead of sadness. I knew that my dark night was over and I had hope for the future.

The Universe made the decision to move me out of that job and my contract was not renewed. I had the summer off to regroup by the pool and look for a new job. Finally, I found an ideal situation working with children in speech and language therapy at a local elementary school. I had unsuccessfully applied for many other positions, but I think Divine guidance led me to the work that was right for me. I enjoyed using my language skills and designing lesson plans for a while, but my metaphysical pursuits were my real passion.

I had seen a psychic during this time who saw me working at a spiritual center coordinating programs and doing my healing work. The idea really appealed to me, but I didn't know how it would manifest. Eventually, I connected with a woman who had an office suite with an empty room. She allowed me to set up my massage table and healing tools. I wasn't too eager to put on programs, but one weekend she had to be out of town and asked me to host the regularly scheduled workshop. I agreed, but I didn't tell anyone about it. Understandably, nobody showed up.

I thought to myself, "This is silly. If I am going to invest the energy into putting on a program, I should have people there to benefit from it." I was now on a mission. I hit the streets marketing a festival featuring speakers, psychics, and healers. The spiritual community came out in full force to support it, and we went into overtime. I started to host these events on a regular basis and created The Spiritual Awareness Network Web site. It was designed to keep people informed about local programs and practitioners. These projects were a lot of work, but I became certain that I was on my path. The many synchronicities that I experienced were signposts along the way.

I would meet people at exactly the right time to fill a need or make a connection. I believe that many of us had agreed to join forces before incarnating. I started to psychically perceive people coming into my life before I met them. It all seemed like a divinely orchestrated dance. Even when I encountered challenges, many felt destined to happen. I have been told by psychics that I would write a book. I didn't know what to write about, but at just the right time, Jahallah entered my life and gave me direction. I now have great clarity, knowing that I am to continue my spiritual work full time, and I am enjoying every minute of it.

Angel of Clarity Prayer

"Mother-Father God, I choose to see clearly. Show me what is true and valuable in your eyes. May all of the dark places in the world be illuminated with light and love. I expect my divine purpose to become clear to me. I will remove any excess clutter from my life that impedes my connection with Spirit. I choose to have clear psychic vision and greater access to wisdom and knowledge. I will share insights that I receive with others for the betterment of mankind. And so it is."

Three ways that I will experience clarity in my life are . . .
1.

2.

3.

IDEAS:

1. Blindfold yourself and sit in the middle of a garden at night.

2. Visit a psychic that has been recommended by someone you trust.

3. Read *Messages to Our Family.*

transition

The greater the obstacle, the more glory in over-coming it.

MOLIERE

Today I would like to speak with you about transition. It would be safe to say that many in the world have already had much experience with this concept. Every day things are changing at a rapid pace. They seem to be moving faster than at any other time in your recorded history. The old is being left behind to make way for the new. Each time this takes place, we must discern if the change is for our higher good or if the old way has value.

I went through a time of transition when I was a child on earth. My mother came to me one day and told me that we were moving from the country to the city. I had never been far from home, and I wasn't sure what to expect. On the day of the move, all of our possessions were loaded into a wagon, and a team of oxen pulled us to our destination. I watched our home disappear in the distance as we headed toward our new life.

I was filled with a sense of loss, yet I had hope that the future would hold many good things. When we arrived in the town, the noise and activity were tremendous. I became a bit nervous as I watched the foreign scene around me. We stopped at a building with tall, stone walls. We went inside and I found that other families were living there. They watched us pass by with our belongings. Occasionally I was greeted with a wave or a smile.

We set up our beds and our cooking utensils in a small room. I was starting to feel sad that we were going to be living in such crowded conditions. My mother came by and gave me a hug of encouragement. Suddenly, a man appeared in our doorway. He seemed intoxicated and was slurring his speech. I was a bit frightened. My father asked the man what he wanted. He said that he had come to welcome us into the building.

To show hospitality, my parents invited him in to share some food. As we sat around our small table, the conversation turned to the business of the neighborhood. "I wanted to let you know that you need to watch out for certain people in this place," the man said. "I hope you never have to encounter the landlord, because he can be harsh. If you are late paying the rent, he will have no mercy." My father thanked him for coming by and showed him to the door.

Later that day, we received a visit from the landlord. He was a tall, well-groomed gentleman with nice manners. He brought us a basket of food as a welcome gift. My mother was grateful for his generosity and made him a special meal. He told us that if we ever needed help to contact him. He reached into his pocket and gave me a wooden toy. It was a dancing bear. I played with it until bed-

time and felt comforted that we had been shown kindness in this new place.

I soon adjusted to the city and often remembered that first day when I received my wooden bear. It was a reminder to me to reach out to people when they were going through difficult changes. A small gesture can make all the difference in someone's life. I would encourage each of you to be aware of these types of situations. If someone is angry or unpleasant or afraid, it is probably due to a transition that is taking place in their life.

I have found that there can also be much joy and enthusiasm when facing life's new challenges. There are always two ways to view something, and we will create our own reality. The angry neighbor viewed the landlord as cruel, but I think that was just the perspective or lens that he was seeing his life through. I imagine you can think of a time in your life when you thought a change would be bad, but many benefits arose from it.

Change is inevitable. If we embrace it, we have the opportunity to see and feel and sense many wonderful things. I am here to share with you some ideas that will help you make changes more easily. First, go within and feel what sensation each choice brings to you. Does one option cause you to feel ill at ease?

If so, make sure this is not due to unfounded fears. Fear of the unknown can block you from many wonderful experiences. Our soul is on a journey of continuous expansion and evolution. We haven't even scratched the surface of what we can accomplish. Don't be afraid to branch out and experience something new.

Spirit communication is a way to explore unknown realms. Your guides can also provide you with information that can make your *transitions smoother. If you don't feel ready for formal spirit communication, that is fine. The still, small voice of your inner guidance will lead you to your destination. You can embrace the changes that are taking place within you as well as in the outer world. That is really the most exciting journey of all. As you reawaken to your true self, a vast array of possibilities will be opened up to you.*

Enjoy these opportunities for change and revel in the growth that is taking place each day. If you have setbacks, do not be alarmed. They are lessons to be learned. They may teach you to shift your perceptions or to choose love instead of fear. Just acknowledge what it has added to your life and move on. Transition need not be difficult, and I am always here to help. Yours forever, Jahallah.

Many people believe that my friend Purusha is an incarnated fairy. She has a fun, enthusiastic personality and offers many uplifting services, such as inspirational speaking. She has a deep love for animals, so she adopted two kittens from an animal shelter and named them Flower and Butterfly. Ten years later she felt that she had made a mistake. Even though Butterfly and Flower were brother and sister, they didn't get along very well. Butterfly never gave Purusha any trouble. He always ate whatever she put down for him. He was easygoing, agreeable, affectionate, and independent. He was quiet and docile, yet he had a playful, mischievous nature.

Flower, on the other hand, was just the opposite. She was temperamental and a fussy eater. Purusha was constantly trying to find the perfect meal for her. She "talked" with a piercing, nonstop wail, which drove Purusha up the wall. The cat was antisocial and spent the entire day hiding in the closet. She would come out only to eat or cruise the backyard at night. She hated being petted and would shake Purusha's hand away. She was always hissing or growling at something or someone, usually her sweet brother. Flower pushed all Purusha's negative buttons, and she spent most of her time trying to control her disappointment and anger.

Butterfly contracted a rare form of lymphatic cancer and passed on. Purusha suffered great sadness. After Butterfly's departure, Flower's behavior got even worse. She started howling in the middle of the night and Purusha could not sleep. Purusha found a new kitten named Sparkle to keep Flower company, hoping this would finally bring peace and happiness to the household. Flower would have nothing to do with Sparkle. As the days went on, Flower's dislike of the kitten became more and more apparent. It was fortunate that the kitten was a tree climber, because Flower, in her senior years, was not.

When Purusha saw Flower sneak up and attack Sparkle when she was sleeping, she knew she had to keep them separated. She set up a residence for Flower in the spare room. Flower then became sick with diarrhea that would not go away. She was diagnosed with pancreatitis. They also found that she had degenerative arthritis in her lower spine and hips. Purusha realized, in retrospect, that this condition was congenital and she had been suffering for years. The cat probably didn't like being petted because it hurt.

Purusha felt very guilty when she learned this news. Her heart and soul could not give up on Flower. She knew she might never be able to get through to this cat and might never have a moment's peace as long as she lived, but there was no way that she could abandon her. She took Flower into the kitchen to enjoy some supper. From that moment on, their relationship shifted. Flower continued to wake Purusha up every night, but her reaction was totally different. Instead of being angry, she held the cat in her arms as it slept. She learned how to pet her where it didn't hurt (her chin, her cheeks, and her ears) and each night she would happily go back to sleep to the sound of purring.

The illness continued to progress and Flower was finally ready to make her transition. As Purusha said good-bye for the last time, she had the most wonderful revelation. She realized that Flower was much more than a pet. She was one of her greatest teachers. She taught her the true meaning of unconditional love. Through this experience of sacrifice and patience, Purusha had come to know the ultimate joy of loving. Purusha will never be without the lessons Flower taught her. She is certainly one of the most important loves of Purusha's life and one of her dearest friends.

Angel of Transition Prayer

"Mother-Father God, I acknowledge that life is filled with changes. These can be met with resistance or acceptance. I choose to overcome challenges with grace and ease. Show me the lessons to be learned in each circumstance, so that I can move forward quickly. I embrace the qualities of patience, trust, healing, and love that come from these experiences. I will focus on the good that comes from transitions, and I will maintain my peace. And so it is."

Three ways that I will experience smooth transitions in my life are . . .

1.

2.

3.

IDEAS:

1. Visit a new city and appreciate cultural diversity.

2. Take flowers to a nursing home and comfort someone in transition.

3. Consider a change you have been resisting and list five reasons why it could be a positive experience.

encouragement

Believe in yourself. Have faith in your abilities.
Without . . . confidence in your own powers, you
cannot be happy or successful.

NORMAN VINCENT PEALE

The focus of today's talk is encouragement. I congratulate you on your efforts to persevere with the tasks you have set before yourself to accomplish in the spiritual realms. I want each person reading this to know that even if life seems to be a constant struggle, great growth is taking place from your willingness to move forward. You are a strong being of light and you came to this earth plane because you knew there was much work to do to help others raise their vibrations. Before entering this incarnation, you each had a plan for advancing your own evolution and the evolution of mankind.

Begin each day by taking an inventory of the ways you can move toward your goals. Know that there are angels in heaven who are rejoicing at each endeavor designed to bring healing to the planet. *Transformation takes place when your mind surrenders to your soul. Please be assured that you will know when this has taken place. The sense of well-being and peace that arises from following your higher guidance is an indicator that you are on the right path.*

If you find yourself discouraged or depressed, ask yourself what blocks to love you are creating in your life. Take action to heal any hurt relationships or situations that have transpired due to unloving thoughts and actions. You are the best judge of your own highest integrity. White lies and little slip-ups need attention as well as the big problems.

Imagine now that your life is in perfect order. How would it look? An easy, peaceful, flowing, graceful existence is available to us at any time. Would you see yourself with a happy spouse and family? Or would you be content to be single but surrounded by a supportive network of friends? Would your career be one that honors yourself and others as well as providing financial rewards? Would your body be healthy and free of toxins? Would you enjoy many opportunities for fun and play? Would you follow your dreams to make each one a reality?

It is done. On the spiritual realm, all things that you desire are already manifest. Bringing them into physical experience takes conscious focus and deliberate action, but it is really quite easy. I am not underestimating the fact that each of you had to grow up in a society where fear consciousness and limiting beliefs were taught. However, you are the best person to teach yourself differently. And the time to do this is now. You don't have to seek after holy men or gurus to teach you what you already know. Go within and ask your higher self to come forward.

The time is now to make your dreams a reality. Expect to be encouraged by others and they will appear. When I was on the earth plane, I wanted to become a writer. Nobody seemed to believe that it was possible for me to accomplish this goal. I became a bit discouraged until one day when I met a man named Josephus. He was knowledgeable about many things. He took me under his wing and taught me about writing and about the mysteries of the universe. He showed me how to convey my thoughts on paper in an easy manner. I didn't have to struggle to find words, but wrote as though I were in a conversation with someone. He encouraged me to share what I had learned with others.

I spent many hours writing manuscripts and pouring all of my thoughts and emotions onto the pages. People started to gather together to hear me read what I had written. The documents started to circulate through the village, and scribes began to make more copies to pass on. Many came to me and said that what I had written had helped them solve problems in their lives. One woman said that my words provided her with encouragement when she was going through a difficult time.

Have a willingness to put your ego aside and live from your heart and soul. Follow your heart and you will overcome obstacles and challenges. Live your life according to what brings you joy and fulfillment. Miracles will occur when you do this. I know that you can create a rewarding life beyond your wildest imagination. I encourage you to love yourself and others today. Peace and blessings, Jahallah.

I was pleasantly surprised that Jahallah had chosen this topic to share with me. He seemed to know what I needed to hear to provide me with encouragement. My husband Larry and I were facing challenges in our marriage. He felt that my energies were moving in another direction, and he had no interest in joining me on the journey. His focus was motor sports, and he was angry that he was unable to purchase better motorcycles and equipment. I was upset by his attitudes and behavior, and he voiced displeasure for mine. I thought about separating because we didn't seem to have one thing in common and we argued a lot.

I knew that the Universe was guiding me, and a Divine plan was unfolding. All I could do was to try my best each day to extend love. I was sure the details would fall into place. I went to my angel journal and drew the card of Choice. Freedom of choice is a valuable gift given to us by our Creator. Everyone needs to take personal responsibility for moving forward or staying where they are. There is no one outside of ourselves to blame for unhappiness or misfortune. We choose our lives and learn from each experience.

I stopped to think about what ways my life would change if I chose to move out of this relationship. I thought about what would be gained and what would be lost. I was grateful that I had encouragement from spirit helpers and friends as I made these choices. As I created a shift within myself, the relationship with my husband began to heal. He started to walk around with a loving expression on his face and would do little things to please me. I felt hopeful and encouraged. He showed a willingness to wait until the money manifested for his purchases.

I continued to work hard, use prosperity affirmations, and send out prayers. My answer came in an unexpected form. We made a financial decision that lowered our monthly mortgage payments and gave us some disposable income. Larry was able to buy his motorcycle, and we paid off our credit cards. I was even able to travel a bit and take some classes to improve my metaphysical skills. I sent out thanks for our abundant lives.

It is easy to have a positive attitude when things are going well, but our challenge is to remain trusting as we go through difficult times. It means a lot when people in our lives give us encouragement. It helps us to maintain confidence in ourselves. You can bolster yourself up by filling your mind with loving thoughts and engaging in uplifting activities. Give encouragement to others and the energy will be returned to you.

Angel of Encouragement Prayer

"Mother-Father God, instead of focusing on changing discouraging situations, I will go within and focus on changing the fears that created them. I know that I am supported by my Creator each step of the way. I know that as I encourage others, the gift will be returned to me. Sacrifice is not a concept understood in the heavenly realms. There is plenty of love, joy, and abundance for everyone. I take this encouraging thought into my life today and I know that all is well."

Three ways that I will experience encouragement in my life
are . . .

1.

2.

3.

IDEAS:

1. Tutor a special needs child and reward their efforts with
   a small gift.

2. Dress up for a night on the town and smile approvingly
   at yourself in the mirror.

3. Give a puppy (or your husband) a pat on the head or a
   good belly rub.

cooperation

There can be hope only for a society which acts as
one big family, not as many separate ones.

ANWAR AL-SADAT

*The message for today will be cooperation. This venture we are
undertaking together is a classic example of cooperation. When
two or more beings join together to create, their synergy makes the
process very powerful. Trying to "go it alone" is not always the
easy path. Remember that there are guides and angels in the heavenly realms available to assist you at all times. Because you are
willing to bring forth spiritual wisdom, you have many beings
ready to support you. Picture a giant kaleidoscope blending and
merging. The image is symbolic of the energies of creation. We are
all one beautiful whole, ever-changing and melding together to
create new beauty in every moment.*

*When I was on the earth plane, I remember an example of co-
operation in my village. There was a great drought and a short-
age of water. One person alone did not have the tools, knowledge,*

and strength to build a well. When we all joined together, the task was accomplished in record time. The well example is analogous of your work. You are tapping into the ever-flowing spring of consciousness and bringing forth information. Together, we will accomplish the goal quickly.

Many people in intimate relationships are at odds because their goals are different and there is a lack of cooperation. Sometimes compromise is needed to reach a place where both parties can work together. Don't be distressed that many marriages seem to be in conflict. Each person has chosen the perfect partner to learn life's lessons. Granted, once those lessons are learned, it could be detrimental to stay in some relationships if there is ongoing abuse or dissension. You can know when it is the right time to move on if you have given your best efforts to lovingly support and forgive the other person.

So many times people leave their marriages with anger and condemnation. More than likely, if this takes place, the life lesson has not been wholly completed. They will probably attract the "same" man or woman into their lives until they can work through the process healthfully and release negative emotions. Practicing cooperation each time you meet someone can turn even simple interactions into holy encounters. Have you ever wondered why there is so much fighting in the world? It is because people are not secure within themselves and feel a need to attack or defend.

We will eventually come to realize that our safety lies in our defenselessness. Currently, world leaders have an extremely difficult time carrying this principle into their global interactions. Many believe that stockpiling weapons and strong-arming others will "protect" them. I know that you do not believe this is the best course of action. You are right to focus on creating a spiritual shift within that would influence the external situation. The "flag waving in the name of destruction," as you called it, may or may not have been some people's attempts to cooperate and keep high intentions. Each person must make those decisions individually. It is not productive to judge. That would only add to the energy of separation.

This story will unfold and all that you can do is play your individual role. Send out as much light as possible to those who are warring within and without. Begin each day with a prayer for peace and it will manifest. Someday, all people will be able to live in love and cooperation. You can experience that now. Blessings to you, my dear one, from your devoted Jahallah.

My husband and I have different opinions about most things, including politics. One night, I returned from a peace rally, and I received a lot of opposition from him. He stated that our "insignificant" antiwar demonstration would have no impact on the world condition. I disagreed and felt that I had to make my voice heard because too many lives were at stake.

I am not usually politically active, however, the military occupation in the Middle East after the events of 9/11 prompted me to become involved. I sent out e-mails advocating peace and kept people informed about gatherings designed to promote cooperation. I was not old enough to participate in the demonstrations during the sixties, but I resonate with that kind of idealism and admire people who were taking a stand for justice.

I attended a local street fair, and I met some people organizing a peace coalition. I signed up to receive notices about their rallies and events. As I walked past the rows of stalls, I encountered one man raging at the Islam students sharing their literature. I asked him why he was so angry, and he rambled a bit about the political climate and "religious differences." I wasn't sure he was grasping the principles underlying his religious dogma, but I blessed him and went on my way.

At the fair, I heard that the president was holding a two-million-dollar fund-raiser in our small town. I felt that I should participate in the peace march. A friend of mine who had been active in the sixties' protests told me stories of tempers flaring and arrests being made. She didn't want to join me at the rally because she didn't want anything to disrupt her home life and family security. I did feel, however, that I should do something. I made a little sign that said, "One God, One People, One World . . . Peace."

I definitely didn't want to be a part of a group "fighting against" everything, but instead hoped to find a group that was "advocating" peace. I drove downtown after work that night and found hundreds of police officers cordoning off the city streets. I could hear the rally by the convention center but had to walk a long way to reach it because of the barricades. I approached the crowd and saw one woman selling T-shirts that read, "A Village in Texas is Missing an Idiot." That was my first indicator of the tone of the gathering.

Some of the chants and signs were very angry. One sign depicted a picture of Bush with a Hitler mustache and the caption: "International Terrorist." People shouted, "Hey, George, you can't hide. We charge you with genocide." There was a group of young people that were getting really pumped up on the adrenaline in the situation. They were drumming and yelling and dancing. A line of police officers in full riot gear held the crowd at bay. A police representative was filming everything as evidence in the event of criminal activity. Many of the young people wore bandanas over their faces to protect their identities.

A couple of girls were dressed like Iraqi women with blood and injuries on their bodies. Some of the boys were cursing, flipping people off, and badgering the police. A girl with a loudspeaker began shrieking, and I could see elderly women plugging their ears. When things got a little unruly, I approached a quiet older woman. We had a conversation about the message being conveyed at this event.

She looked at me blankly when I made a comment about the counterproductive dynamic that was created by meeting violence and negativity with the same energies. She looked around and said, "This is actually a fairly reserved event. I do think that passion is necessary to get the point across. We need more people to come out and let their voices be heard." I agreed with that, but moved to the quiet side of the crowd. I tried to speak with a policeman to get his opinion. He had "no comment," but referred me to the public relations representative.

The wealthy participants of the fund-raiser began to emerge from the building. One person called out, "Shame on you! Two million for tyranny." A pro-Bush faction showed up on the scene and started a screaming match with the protestors. The police photographer moved his position, feeling this was the most volatile situation. Fortunately, the blazer-clad Republicans were ignored after this began. They were able to reach their cars in the parking lot safely.

A group of about eighteen people from the dinner passed by me. The women wearing cocktail dresses and fine jewelry carried their floral centerpieces. The nine men were talking animatedly on their cell phones, and at first I thought they were security escorts. As they walked by, I heard one man's conversation. "Hi honey, how was your day at school?" This was a reminder that the "opposition" were just people with different opinions doing the best that they could with the values they had been taught.

I decided to speak with some women who gathered every week in front of the library in silent vigil. They were members of the "Women in Black" who demonstrated for justice and peace. I was given a flyer describing their beliefs. It read: "We stand in silence, because words alone cannot express the tragedy that wars and hatred bring. We stand in black, mourning for lives broken or lost through violence . . . in all wars. We stand in witness, to the suffering of victims of violence all over the world. We stand in solidarity, with people . . . who struggle for justice and peace. We stand convinced that the world's citizens can learn the difference between justice and vengeance, and can call world leaders into accountability to employ non-violent means to resolve conflicts."

Those words were very powerful. I knew that each person's efforts would make a difference in changing the mass consciousness. I loved meeting people who understood the importance of working together to create peace on the planet. I went home that night inspired to work at creating cooperation in my relationships.

I asked my husband to attend a New Age expo with me. He agreed to take me since I did not enjoy navigating the crowded streets of Los Angeles. One couple was selling peace sign bumper stickers made up of world flags. I bought one to place on my car window as a symbol of global oneness. I had a comfortable feeling in these gatherings and felt like I had found "my people." However, my husband was restlessly rolling his eyes and acting impatient, so we left the expo arguing. As I continue to do my inner work, perhaps someday my husband and I will cooperate more and agree to disagree peacefully.

Angel of Cooperation Prayer

"Mother-Father God, I allow my life to flow effortlessly as I cooperate with You. I am here to fulfill a role that was especially designed for me. As I work with others in love and harmony, those goals will be accomplished easily. I release all dissension in my life and all need to attack or defend. I will extend myself to be of assistance to those in need. I am safe and supported by the

Universe. I am surrounded by people who work together for the common good. And so it is."

Three ways that I will experience cooperation in my life are:
1.

2.

3.

IDEAS:
1. Join a group working on a charitable cause.

2. Acknowledge another person's point of view as impor-
    tant, even if you disagree with him.

3. Organize a noncompetitive game for children on a
    playground.

healing

The healing of God's son is all the world is for.
That is the only purpose the Holy Spirit sees in it
and thus the only one it has.

A COURSE IN MIRACLES

The need for healing comes in a variety of forms. Some may feel pain in their physical bodies. Some may feel heartsick and lack wholeness on mental and emotional levels. You can be assured that if you heal your spirit, the rest will be restored. We are energetic beings, and all illness originates on the subtle levels before it manifests in the body. We see a great many people trying to medicate and operate, while the source of the problem is ignored. There have been many good books written about the body-mind connection that can provide you with valuable tools and information.

What I would like to focus on today is teaching you how to release energies that are not benefiting your health and well-being. Take a look at your life and notice areas that are causing you discomfort. Examine any ways that you are not acting in a loving manner. Notice if you are giving an extraordinary amount of energy to mundane concerns. Then try to imagine yourself in a place and time where none of these things matter anymore. You will find yourself in the present moment.

Use this moment to ask your Creator to run energy through your body to clear out blocks and chords. Pull in cosmic energy through your crown chakra and soak up earth energy through the soles of your feet. If you are experiencing pain in any part of your body, send it loving acceptance. You have many tools and helpers available to assist you in the process of healing. Seek them out and utilize them.

A meditation that is useful in shifting your energy field is called the "Circle of Love." Take a few minutes to call to mind everyone in your life. They can be family members, acquaintances, or people you pass on the street. Do not exclude anyone. Send each individual thoughts of love and blessings. You will find that your mind-set and energy field will shift and the positive feelings will return to you multiplied.

Health is a choice. You must relinquish all attempts to use your body in an unloving manner. If you are ingesting toxic substances, reconsider this practice because the consequences can be severe. If you are harboring feelings of resentment or anger, you must release them or they will take their toll. Some people choose to be unwell because it takes their attention away from issues that they do not want to face. Be assured that you can run, but you can't hide. Eventually, you will need to bring light to all areas of your life that you have kept hidden.

Because you are reading this book, I would assume that you are tired of wasting time in activities that are not conducive to your health and growth. You are seeking ways to help yourself make progress along your spiritual path. You are going in the right direction. When reunion with your true self is your main focus, the rest of your life will fall into place. You still may experience challenges, but as you stay focused on your connection with the Divine, life will become easier.

Health problems or dis-ease can be great catalysts for change. Don't judge yourself harshly if you have not yet found the way to heal yourself completely. Ask yourself what you can learn from your present situation. Implement the changes necessary to achieve what you really want. It is a continuous process, and your diligence will be rewarded.

When I was a boy in a tiny village, I came across an old gentleman by the side of the road. He was coughing and hacking so violently that I was worried he would not recover. I gave him a sip of my water, and he eventually regained his composure. He told me that he had taken a long journey in search of his daughter. He had lost touch with her many years ago. He wanted to bid her farewell before he journeyed into the next world. I asked for the girl's name and he told me.

"I know her," I said. "I will take you to her." We traveled together to the place I had last seen the young woman. We asked around, but nobody knew where she was. We were told that she might be at one of her favorite spots. It was a natural spring that produced drinking water for the village. We made our way to this location and saw her sitting along the water's edge. She was filling flasks with the sweet, cool water.

When she turned and saw the old man before her, she let out a gasp of surprise. She tentatively approached him. "Daughter, I am so sorry for the unkind things I said to you before our last parting," he told her. "I spoke from a place of anger and my words did not reflect the feelings in my heart." She gave him a gracious smile and offered him a cup of the water to drink. I left them sitting by the spring, enjoying a peaceful silence.

I heard that the old man made his transition surrounded by loved ones. His illness did not plague him, and he passed his days in relative comfort. Dear ones, there is no reason for you to live your lives in pain. When you are unafraid to find the source of your problems, you will be able to heal them. Fearlessly shine love into every corner of your life and you will be healed. Take good care, Jahallah.

In the course of my work finding practitioners for workshops and festivals, I met a dedicated lightworker named Carolyn Kaufman. She offered a wide variety of classes and services, and she had great enthusiasm for her spiritual path. At one of the workshops, she shared her story of healing. Unfortunately, she had led a very dysfunctional childhood and experienced emotional and sexual abuse. This created very unhealthy patterns in her life. She was extremely insecure, shy, and fearful. However, she was determined to prove herself to the world. At age twenty-one, she had a good job at a courthouse and was putting herself through court reporting school. She commuted an hour and a half each day to work, school, and home. It was a very demanding and exhausting lifestyle. She felt that she could never do enough or be enough. She was leading a very stressful life and was heading down a path of self-destruction.

She began feeling ill and started to miss more and more work and school. She could not keep up with the pace that she had created. She was constantly seeing doctors, yet they were not finding anything significantly wrong with her. After two and a half years of this, she was diagnosed with cancer. After six months of harsh, conventional treatments, she was ready to get back to her life. Carolyn started back to work and school only to end up sick again, this time with lupus. This was actually more devastating because it felt like a life sentence. She was told that she would be sick and on medication for the rest of her life. She was told that she would not be able to have any children. She was given a huge list of what she could and could not do. At twenty-four years of age, this was extremely overwhelming.

At age twenty-five, Carolyn got pregnant with the first of her healthy children. She started to question the predictions of the doctors. Maybe she didn't have to experience the picture they had painted for her. At that time, she was introduced to alternative and holistic medicine. She learned Chi-Gong, Tai-Chi, and went to a doctor of homeopathy. She also had treatments in acupuncture and pranic healing. Most importantly, she found Louise Hay's book *You Can Heal Your Life*. She started to understand her life in a whole new way.

Carolyn began realizing that everything was a message, and if she understood the message and learned the lesson, she would no longer need the experience. She began healing and forgiving and releasing destructive patterns from her past. She also went to work on her thoughts. She would plug in positive affirmations whenever she found herself thinking unhealthy thoughts. At the same time, she learned pranic healing and began cleansing her energy field twice daily. Within thirty days of working on her thoughts and energy, her symptoms were gone! She discontinued her medication and has never needed to use it again.

These experiences started a whole new journey for Carolyn and led her to her true passions in life. She learned how powerful it is to let go of the victim mentality and begin taking responsibility for her every thought and action. She learned to see her past challenges as steppingstones and as gifts that brought about a tremendous amount of spiritual growth. She learned that every experience she journeyed through made her a more complete person and helped fill her with compassion. Her worst days now are better than her best days of her past. She lives a very happy and fulfilling life. She may still experience ups and downs, but she has learned to appreciate each experience as a gift, even the ones she doesn't like. Each one is an opportunity for growth.

Since then, she has been helping to empower others to create the life of their dreams. She teaches people to understand the messages that their bodies and experiences are sharing with them. She became a certified spiritual counselor, intuitive reader, and healer. She is very dedicated to raising her children with life-affirming spiritual principles.

Through her own personal journey with cancer and lupus, she has transformed her life. In addition to teaching healing and meditation, she works with Indigo and Crystal children. She created the Web site www.thechildrenoftoday.org and provides invaluable resources and counseling for parents and teachers. Carolyn's story of healing continues to inspire others and motivate them to make changes to improve their own lives.

Angel of Healing Prayer

"Mother-Father God, I send forth gratitude for the healing that is taking place in my life. I see myself as whole and healthy. I acknowledge You as the source of healing energy and the life force that sustains me. I ask for assistance from the angels, ascended masters, and divine spiritual beings who were created to help me along this journey. I pray to be guided back to my true state of perfection and communion with the Divine. And so it is."

Three ways that I will experience healing in my life are . . .

1.

2.

3.

IDEAS:

1. Shop at a Whole Foods or cooperative market and buy organic products.

2. Visit a health spa and indulge in a detoxification regime.

3. Give out seven hugs in one day.

adventure

Adventure is not outside; it is within.

DAVID GRAYSON

Life is an adventure. Every new day holds unlimited possibilities for joy and growth. If you are living in a routine, try to think of one way to break out of old boundaries and try something new. Children are in a state of joy and wonder as they go through their daily activities. Everything is new and interesting. Try to recapture some of that youthful enthusiasm and explore life from a different perspective. It could be as simple as trying a new gourmet food or dance step. As you make efforts to broaden your horizons, new vistas will appear everywhere.

Have you ever had the feeling that something exciting was going to happen? When you agree to move past your comfort zone, it will. When I was a young boy, I went on a trek to the Himalayas. It was the most exciting adventure of my life. There were beautiful views and powerful energy spots to experience. As I hiked through the mountain passes, I would encounter hidden glens where I would rest and connect with the nature spirits. I could hear them whisper in my ear.

One day, a stolid little elf presented himself to me. He was good-natured but concerned about the way that man had been invading the homes of his people. Sometimes they would tear through the brush to forge trails and leave destruction in their wake. He encouraged me to be gentle with the land as I passed through. Communing with nature in new and different ways will add depth to your life experience. You may be able to tune into the realms of the fairies, elementals, and devas. These beings are not simply part of ancient folklore, but are living creatures who play integral roles in maintaining our environment.

You started today's session with enthusiasm even before you knew the topic. We know that it is one of your heart's desires to visit power places all over the world. You will be able to manifest this dream. You will write about the transformational spiritual adventures that you have on your journeys. I ask each person now to find something that triggers that kind of excitement. Make a game plan of how you can reach your goal, and take action toward achieving it each day. Mark your calendar, designating a special day for adventure.

Early man wanted to see what would happen when two stones were rubbed together. That simple experiment produced fire, which became an invaluable tool. You never know what discoveries you can make unless you try something new. It is also amazing to see what can be accomplished on unseen levels when you experiment with energy. Mankind is finding new ways to heal and perceive psychically every day. As you explore your inner world, you will find hidden treasures. You have the ability within you to transform matter and transcend the laws of physics. Jesus and other masters have tapped into many of these inherent gifts.

Suppose you were lost in a jungle. What emotions would arise? Would you feel ill equipped to survive? Or would you relish the new opportunity to extend yourself beyond your normal abilities? In your daily life, you choose between these two extremes every day. Many times we keep ourselves protected and closed off so that we don't have to take risks that might fail. This may help you feel safe, but embracing change is what makes you grow. As you go to work or run errands, be conscious of each action and interpersonal exchange. Could you extend yourself a little bit more to improve your communications and connections to other people? Could you experiment with a new form of artistic or creative expression? When you do this, you will tap into the realms of Spirit for inspiration.

Don't be afraid to sing out loud or fingerpaint. Try something new even though you might not be "good at it." Eliminate value judgments and just be in the moment. Life is a grand adventure. Allow yourself to dive in headfirst, and you will be buoyed up by your guides and angels. Open your lines of communication with them, and ask for assistance when you are treading in uncharted territory. You are not alone in this journey. As you reach out, you will be one step closer to discovering your true self. That is the most exciting adventure of all. Wishing you fun and excitement, Jahallah.

It's true that I love to travel, and it is my goal to visit spiritual places all over the world. I decided to visit Sedona, Arizona for my first adventure. I heard that the town was called the "heart chakra" of the earth and was told that it was a metaphysical mecca. I was not disappointed. The landscape was so beautiful that it took my breath away. I spent a lot of time hiking through the red rocks and enjoying the quiet. On my first day in town, there was a light snowfall. That didn't slow me down a bit. I reveled in the sparkling beauty all around. The next day the sun came out, and all of the vistas were transformed with dazzling colors.

I had an appointment with a shaman in Jerome several miles away. It was fun visiting the little town with a rich paranormal history. The healer's home was high on a cliff. I climbed the long staircase and was welcomed into a warm, cozy room as the snow fell gently outside. He did some energy work with me. When he went to "other worlds" to get information, he told me a story that brought out some strong emotions.

He saw an image of me being crucified, and my loved ones were at the foot of the cross. He said I was crying out, "Why do you crucify me?" For some reason it made me chuckle, and then it made me sad. I couldn't figure out what energy he was picking up on. It might have been a past life, or it might have been a symbol of something in my subconscious. Since I was studying the *Course in Miracles* at that time, I kept thinking, "It can only be myself who I crucify." I felt a release and a feeling of lightness after the session.

Later that day I took a jeep tour through the canyons of Sedona. The driver was well versed in Native American folklore and culture. I visited vortexes and especially liked the one by Oak Creek. I went to a metaphysical center and thought it would be lovely to work in such a setting. The store was filled with crystals and inspirational gifts. A stream flowed outside the back door, and there was a lovely meditation garden.

I visited another place that had a sound chamber. I reclined in a pyramid-shaped bed while music was piped in. The experience was designed to take you into other realms, but for me, it was just relaxing. I had a good psychic reading and healing from talented practitioners, and I felt totally uplifted and renewed by these experiences. The energy was so high that I didn't eat much at all. I bought healthy foods at the grocery store and felt great.

I wanted to make Sedona my yearly pilgrimage in the spring. It was a great place to find people who "spoke my language." The opportunities for experiencing the wonders of nature were limitless. I heard stories of people connecting with the angels, fairies, and devas there. My only "close encounter" was connecting with the water spirits when I accidentally fell into Oak Creek. I had been told that the water contained healing properties, and it did eliminate an annoying skin condition that I had at the time.

It's always fun to be able to take trips to places with high energy, but we can also manifest those sensations within ourselves at any time. As we venture inward, we can create relaxation and regeneration. There are unlimited avenues to explore within the mind and spirit. Our imagination, dreams, and meditations can be developed to take us on amazing journeys. Enjoy the ride!

Angel of Adventure Prayer

"Mother-Father God, I greet each day with enthusiasm as I prepare for wonderful adventures. I am eager to explore new frontiers in my inner and outer worlds. I know that the way will be prepared for me and I will be safe and protected at all times. Because I am willing to grow, I will find the perfect venues to unleash my highest potential. I will find much joy in my life and live each day to the fullest. I am grateful for the many blessings from my Creator. And so it is."

Three ways that I will experience adventure in my life are . . .
1.

2.

3.

IDEAS:
1. Open a travel guide at random and visit that destination.

2. Perform a ritual in the mountains to connect with the animal and nature spirits.

3. Visit a foreign restaurant and eat something you have never tried before.

safety

There is no time, no place, no state where God is
absent. There is nothing to be feared.

A COURSE IN MIRACLES

*Imagine that you are on a deserted island. There is no one to pro-
vide you with company or entertainment or support. Would you
embrace this solitude or resist it? Would you feel safe and secure
despite the absence of material things or other people? Becoming
comfortable with yourself and knowing yourself will bring you
the feelings of safety you desire. As you clear out all of the debris
that makes you uncomfortable, you will find the shining light of
wholeness coming through.*

*How would you feel if hostile people arrived on the island?
Would you begin a pattern of attack and defense? Or would you
be able to send them unconditional love and acceptance? What
coping mechanisms would you use? Would you make more effort
to connect with your spiritual helpers? Great prophets and psychics in your history developed their skills when they were put into*

situations of deprivation. The demands of the flesh became too much, and they went inward for solace and connection to Spirit.

You are at a crossroads in your life. You are beginning a journey that will lead you to a new paradigm. We want to make sure you are ready when this shift appears. Will you depend on the things of the world to support you, or will you know that your strength lies within? Practicing meditation and spirit communication now will prepare you for what lies ahead. You will be guided to safe places, and you will know what steps to take on your path.

When I was a boy of about nineteen, I knew an old woman who tended a flock of sheep. She was very concerned about keeping them protected from predators. She believed that she would not be able to survive if she experienced any kind of loss. She worried and fussed over the animals daily. She never gave herself time to relax or tend to her own needs. She became sick with a fever one day and was drowsing under a tree. A wolf came by and went after one of her most cherished lambs. She became paralyzed with fear and was too weak to defend herself. She made a small commotion, but the wolf sensed that he was in command of the situation and continued to take what he wanted.

Break free of your dependence upon material things so that if you ever lose them, you will not be devastated. Also, each time you are tempted to find temporary gratification in yet another acquisition, stop for a moment and see if you can go within for the solace that you are seeking. You may go ahead and buy what it is you desire for its usefulness to you, but don't depend on it for happiness, fulfillment, or security.

When you attempt to make a transition between earth consciousness and spirit consciousness, you may notice some seeming obstacles on your way. They are opportunities to apply the principles I have been teaching you and to transcend the illusion. You are about to embark on something totally new and uncharted. You know deep within that you have the map that will lead you to the treasures you seek. Spiritual disciplines will help you arrive more quickly at your destination.

Prayer and meditation will keep your link with Spirit strong. Connect with your inner guidance in the way that is comfortable. Don't compare your experiences with others because you will find the best way for you. Because you have a willingness to grow, Spirit is meeting you halfway. We stretch out our hands to help pull you up. Take your place on the throne of awareness. There is no need to struggle.

Listen to your higher self say, "Believe that I am with you always and will never forsake you." You are safe and secure just as you are. Your spirit is eternal and indestructible. Detach yourself from the negative actions of other people and remain firm in your conviction that you are safe and protected. Connect with that quality that does not change and fade, as do the things in the external realm. You are irreplaceable in the eyes of God. You will be cared for at all times. Reconnect with your truth, Jahallah.

I channeled Jahallah's portion of this book first and then settled down to the task of finding anecdotes from my own life that reflected the lessons. I reached this chapter and wondered how to proceed. The Universe sent me an answer that

I couldn't ignore. A jury duty summons came in the mail, and I was preparing to report to the courthouse. I wondered how I would respond in this situation because of my metaphysical beliefs. I wasn't looking forward to being in the position of judging someone and being responsible for their punishment. The city didn't need me for service after all, but three days later I was put into the position of judging a person who had committed a crime.

I was at the store by myself, preparing for a crystal bowl concert in the evening. I was in the office and heard rustling in the main showroom. I was about to greet my "customer," but instead found a man with his hands in our cash register. He grabbed the contents and shoved them into his pockets. I said, "Please don't do this." I was feeling a bit unnerved but remained relatively calm.

He charged toward the exit, yelling at the top of his lungs in an attempt to scare me away. I went to the door as he fled and yelled out some ineffective remark about the "karmic consequences" of his actions. He responded with a few obscenities. I suppose my metaphysical musings were lost on him. I called the police, and they responded with a helicopter and patrol cars. I gave them quite a few details about his appearance, and they found a suspect who resembled the description. As the officer was driving me to the place where they were holding this person, I was asking for assistance from all of my guides and angels. I wasn't comfortable with holding somebody else's fate in my hands. I didn't want to make any mistakes. I knew that universal law would take care of the energy exchange, but at that moment I had to do my "civic duty."

The suspect was taken out of the patrol car and he matched my description of clothing, hair, etc. However, his face was fleshier, and it was obviously not the thief. We returned to the store, and I continued to prepare for the concert. I think the crystal bowls had a soothing effect on me. I still wasn't in a place of fear, but I was rather numb and saddened. I had never had cause to believe the world was unsafe. I had just finished writing chapters in my book assuring others that we were always protected. Did this incident put holes in my belief system? A woman at the concert said, "You will never be the same after this. You have lost your innocence, and you will use this experience as a touchstone in your future decisions and beliefs."

I had to stop and wonder about our safety because the store owner had been robbed several months earlier. A woman came into the shop and gathered up many books and gifts. She then pulled out a gun and demanded the owner's purse and the money in the register. The thief made her lie down on the ground as she held the gun to her head. My employer thought that she was going to die and was praying fervently and making peace with herself. She wasn't harmed, however, and the woman took the phones and drove away in a car.

After this, a security system was installed, but when I was robbed, the alarm didn't work. I lost several minutes of time while I awaited a response from the security company. Fortunately, we had recently emptied the cash register and the thief ended up with some spare change and register receipts. Our major loss was the feeling of vulnerability that these incidents created. It was frustrating to think that while we were dedicating ourselves to building a gathering place for Spirit and healing, these people were coming in to destroy part of our creation. However, I was not going to let them take away the nonmaterial treasures that we had created. The spiritual qualities that we teach and share could not be taken away. I was not going to relinquish trust in the goodness of the Universe.

I posted a quote by Emerson in the store office that read, "The wise man in the storm prays to God, not for safety from danger, but for deliverance from fear." I didn't want to live my life with suspicion and panic buttons and alarm systems. I wanted to believe that people are good, and there is no reason that I should be afraid. Some have accused me of having my head in the sand and being out of touch with reality. It is true that I cannot tolerate watching violence in the media, and I don't engage in conversations about the atrocities that happen all over the planet. I was secure in believing that my little corner of the world was safe and filled with beings of light.

I am still going to maintain that belief. The robber did not harm me, and I lived to write the story in this book. I have a life filled with all of the material possessions that I need. I have a renewed dedication to share what I believe to be spiritual truths. I know that as I shift my consciousness, it will have an influence on those who still think they must steal and harm to have their needs met.

Angel of Safety Prayer

"Mother-Father God, it is a comfort to know that I am safe in your loving protection at all times. My Spirit is indestructible and infinite. I live each day knowing that all will be well. I go within to gain a stronger connection with my true self. I am never alone. My angels, guides, and loved ones are close by, ready to give me support. Even though the process of my life may contain challenges, I will have strength, knowing that I am safe. And so it is."

Three ways that I will experience safety in my life are . . .
1.

2.

3.

IDEAS:
1. Have a conversation with a street person.

2. Become a pen pal with someone in prison and share up-lifting ideas.

3. Send blessings and light to a passing police officer.

support

> Surround yourself with only people who are going
> to lift you higher.
>
> OPRAH WINFREY

*Imagine that you are on an ocean shore. The tide is flowing in,
washing over you. The sun is shining brightly, warming your skin.
The wind is gently caressing your body. The energy from Mother
Earth is nurturing you. Just as the elements of nature sustain you,
know that you are always supported by Spirit. As you become still
and aware of the present moment, the sensation of support will
appear more real to you.*

Traditionally, when people think of the word support, *they
think of lifting up and carrying a burden. It is not a burden for the
Universe to sustain you. It was designed to do so. In turn, you extend love and support to others and the cycle continues. Your burden does not need to be heavy. It may be perceived in this manner,
but that is not true in reality. You can worry and hurry yourself
into depletion, but all you really need to do is draw on the energy*

that is readily available to you. There are masters who have developed this ability to such a degree that they do not need food or water for sustenance.

As you stopped typing to experience what this might feel like, you were taken over by a sense of calmness and well-being. You had a knowing that the love in the Universe was buoying you up. You were light and everything was easy. We only make life difficult when we believe that it is. Butterflies are creatures that are lifted up and supported by the elements. Their lives are fleeting yet filled with powerful awareness. Their journey reminds us to be in reverence of each sacred moment.

As the butterfly goes about its day, it is a source of radiance to everyone who witnesses it. You can do this as well, touching lives and leaving your mark of beauty. Think also of the metamorphosis that a butterfly must go through to attain his wings. It is a process that cannot be rushed. The cycle is in perfect order. So, too, is your life plan. Each interaction is designed to help you learn and grow. Don't be worried if something is "taking too long" to manifest. The wisdom of the Universe is guiding you, and the timing will be perfect.

Many times people support each other because there will be a payoff. Other times it is because they are giving unconditionally, without attachments to outcome. We see that many relationships are like a bargaining game. If you give this to me, I will give that to you. This dynamic blocks the natural flow of universal energy. Would the sun only shine on those that it thought deserving? Of course not. Your Creator gives willingly to anyone who will accept the gifts. Because you have asked for my support, I am here. It is that simple.

When I was on the earth plane, I received assistance from my spirit guides. A group of young men would gather periodically in the town square to give public speeches. I found that my discourses were the most eloquent when I was in tune with my Divine helpers. People would ask me questions, and sometimes I gave them information that I had not previously known. I was happy to be able to provide them with knowledge that awakened the truth within them.

You are working to bring through wisdom that will help others, and that is a worthy endeavor. Be assured that you will be supported each step of the way. Planetary changes are making it necessary to bring through information that will help people understand themselves and the laws of the Universe. Pay attention to the voice of guidance within you. It is not the voice that is replaying radio tunes or rehashing arguments. Your quiet voice might say, "Stop, listen. I will help you."

You are an irreplaceable part of Creation, and there is no possible way for you to be lost. At times, it may seem as though you are fumbling in the dark, but be assured that the light is there when you are ready to see it. Yes, listening takes practice to receive clear messages. Persevere in your efforts to know God more intimately. In this process, you will come to know yourself. We are All that is. Once you realize it, it will be impossible for you to experience lack. You are supported, dear one. Remember to support yourself, Jahallah.

In school, I was somewhat of an overachiever, always striving to get perfect grades and approval. I found myself reliving that energy when I was organizing festivals. I worked compulsively, following up on every idea for marketing and taking care of endless details. I invested a lot of time and energy into these projects and was disappointed if the financial rewards were small. Some days I would just break even, and I had to go within and evaluate my prosperity consciousness. I would say all of the "right" affirmations about abundance, but what was there inside of me that was blocking the flow of money? I was determined to find out so that I could help create a more prosperous life for my family.

My husband Larry was the person who prompted me to start writing a book. He said, "I don't know many people who have your gift with language. You should write a book about your spiritual ideas and experiences." I was somewhat surprised by this because he had not given me much validation regarding my metaphysical pursuits in the past. I said, "You have always acted like this work is not important." He said, "I don't think it is, but I think it will sell." He later went on to soften his response. "I don't mean that it is not important, I just haven't taken the time to explore it like you have." He assures me that he will do just that when he is too old to ride motorcycles.

Everyone has their own path and will find their way back to the Source eventually. I had to give credit to my husband for supporting me for so long. He worked hard every day, and we had a comfortable home. Granted, he spent a lot of money on his hobbies, but we always had what we needed. Even though he sometimes harassed me about my income, he continued to pay the bills and allowed me to follow my heart. I think we probably made some sort of agreement for mutual support before incarnating. Even though we are exact opposites, we both have unique gifts to contribute to the partnership.

I have some wonderful like-minded people in my life who have always supported me. My friends Glory Ward and Trez Ibrahim were very encouraging over the years and helped out when I coordinated events. Most of the people I met in the metaphysical community were very loving. They showed me a lot of appreciation for the work I did. My grandparents, parents, and brother made themselves available to help me whenever I needed it. Even though I come from a traditional upbringing, my family encouraged me as I explored spirituality and found the path that was right for me.

I am indescribably grateful for the contributions that my guide Jahallah has made in my life. It never failed to amaze me that he conveyed just the right anecdote or guidance that I needed to help me shift my perceptions. Time and time again, he would provide me with reminders that there are many perspectives and many ways to handle each situation. Release and surrender were key themes in this process. He never counseled me to sit back and expect the Universe to hand me life on a silver platter, but prompted me to take spiritually directed action. When I found myself getting caught up in frantic activity, I would be reminded not to lose sight of my inner peace and direction. He encouraged me to ask for Divine assistance often.

My angels and healing guides were active in my everyday activities to inspire me and raise my energy. They all contributed to the creation of this book. I know that the process I went through to bring this project into manifestation has helped me to grow and evolve. It's nice to know that we have support along our journey.

It feels good to provide support for others as well. In my networking endeavors, I am directed by strong inner promptings to assist people in their spiritual work. I provide leads for practitioners and direct clients to the services they need. It wasn't my intention to create a support network, but it unfolded effortlessly and has been very successful. I know that as this lightworkers' network grows, many lives will be transformed and consciousness on the planet will be lifted.

Angel of Support Prayer

"Mother-Father God, I marvel at the many ways that I am supported by the Universe. I extend gratitude to the people and spiritual beings who have helped me along my journey. I know that I will be given opportunities to share this energy with others. I envision a network of lightworkers spanning the globe to create healing and greater spiritual awareness. May we remember that we are all One and as we help others, we help ourselves. And so it is."

Three ways that I will experience support in my life are . . .

1.

2.

3.

IDEAS:

1. Make a contribution to a new charitable organization.

2. Accompany your spouse on an outing that interests him and act like you are enjoying yourself.

3. In the next birthday card you send, write five reasons why the recipient is special.

participation

> Knowing is not enough; we must apply. Willing is
> not enough; we must do.
>
> GOETHE

If you have chosen to incarnate during these times of global change, you probably had an important reason for coming to this planet. There is too much to be accomplished now for you to sit on the sidelines and watch life pass you by. I would encourage you to participate in healing and uplifting the consciousness of your society. Don't be concerned if you feel ill prepared to make a significant impact. What you do in your small corner of the world affects the entire society. Become clear about what it is that you can contribute, and take action to do it.

By taking control of your life, you can eliminate wasting time with useless drama. Think about the scenarios that are playing out now in your life. Which ones are not productive? Can you think of a dysfunctional relationship or activity that has kept you tied up? Is it really necessary to fuel the fires by investing your emotion in them? It takes a strong, focused effort to separate yourself from these situations and practice unconditional love instead of blame and justification. Think of how much energy you would have to spare if you were not perpetuating constant dialogues and activities to attack or defend.

Take time now to connect with your higher self and ask for guidance on how to ascend above these energies. People usually know exactly how to solve their dilemmas, but hesitate to make changes for many reasons. A counselor could advise you, but your higher self will cut to the chase and give direct guidance. Ask yourself, "What action can I take right now that would create a shift in my life? What can I do to heal myself?"

During one lifetime on earth, I was visiting a neighboring village. I stopped by the home of the magistrate who was embroiled in a campaign to make some changes in the local government. There were some policies in effect that were not serving the needs of the people. He could have allowed the status quo to continue. It would have been more convenient for him. However, he chose to extend himself in an effort to improve the quality of life for everyone.

I cannot say that his road was easy or that he did not meet with opposition. Many people were averse to change, but in the long run they were glad that someone took the initiative to act. He forgot about the pain and hardship when the new order was in place. It will be the same on the earth plane when these current transitions and "growing pains" have passed. A new age is approaching, and some are resisting their own evolution. They are acting out in destructive ways. This is no cause for alarm because the final resolution will be in favor of the light.

In the meantime, it is up to each individual to take action to help those who are dragging their feet. You don't need to proselytize or coerce, just lead by example and suggestion. This lifetime is a valuable gift. I would encourage you not to waste it. Take chances and stretch yourself. Know that you have the support of your spiritual helpers. We will lift you up if you fall. We will traverse time and space and come to your aid. Don't be afraid to get back up and run. Seize the day, Jahallah.

While I was hosting a metaphysical gathering, I received a psychic reading that said I was going to be more active in teaching. People would expect me to be in a position of leadership, whether I wanted to or not. I definitely was more comfortable being behind the scenes. I had attempted public speaking a couple of times but did not really enjoy it. However, I always follow my inner guidance when doing my spiritual work, even though it might challenge me. I knew that the message was too important to let my ego concerns create blocks.

I agreed to a speaking engagement and asked my friend Chantal to accompany me. I knew the crowd would enjoy her singing talents, and I could tie my message into the theme of her music. Our message was about creating peace in our lives and around the world. The words of one song had really impacted me when I first heard them. I was in the midst of a festival, busily coordinating appointments for psychic readings and healings while Chantal was singing. The energy in the room shifted, and my eyes started to fill with tears even before I heard the words. I was strongly impacted by the powerful meaning the song was conveying. She gave me a reminder of the importance of participating in life and embracing the oneness of all mankind.

Her lyrics were inspired by the aftermath of 9/11. They made me realize that there wasn't time to waste and that it was time to get to work on healing the planet. Many times, tragedy inspires and motivates us to take action.

Her song encouraged people to participate more fully in the process of their evolution. She sang about the pain and suffering that arise when we engage in war. She gave voice to the people crying out, "No more anger in our name!" She foretold of nations rising above division and enemies joining hands. She saw less competition and more cooperation in the world. She felt that peace would manifest as each of us contributed our gifts to help each other. Love would be the energy that could create the change we wanted to see.

I have never been a political person, but peace advocacy is important to me. I admire spiritual leaders such as Marianne Williamson, James Twyman, and Neale Donald Walsch, who are actively working to make changes on a global level. Chantal flew up to Oregon to join Neale's first Humanity's Team gathering. I know she is going to make a big impact on the world, sharing her message through her music.

After a couple of months of writing, I slowed down because I wasn't sure what step to take next. During a healing session, an intuitive told me that Jahallah was encouraging me to move forward because my guides had more books that they wanted to write. I could feel the heat of his presence and felt that I was being supported and guided. When I finally made myself sit down at the computer, I was always given direction. All the Divine needs is a little willingness on our part. We shouldn't let our feelings of fear or inadequacy hold us back from taking action.

Everyone has a role to fulfill in the Divine plan. Even if you are not an extroverted person, you can always do inner work on behalf of the mass consciousness. When you strengthen your connection with Spirit, it will impact everyone else for the better because we are all One. There are many ways that we can each contribute to the evolution of humanity. Do what comes naturally and share your inherent gifts.

Angel of Participation Prayer

"Mother-Father God, I am fortunate to have been given the gift of life, and I intend to make the most of it. I will participate fully in manifesting and loving and growing. I choose to utilize all of my inherent spiritual gifts, such as communication, intuition, and healing. I am thankful for the myriad ways that I can express my creativity and make a positive impact on humanity. I know that it is time to get in touch with what is truly valuable in my world and share it with others. And so it is."

Three ways that I will experience participation in my life are . . .

1.

2.

3.

IDEAS:

1. Write a letter to the editor with positive ideas for creating change in your community.

2. Lend a hand with an organization like Habitat for Humanity.

3. Complete a task today that you have been putting off.

versatility

Never tell people how to do things . . . they will
surprise you with their ingenuity.

GEORGE S. PATTON

*Sometimes people become stuck in one place because of resistance
to change. Perhaps this is due to fear of the unknown, perhaps it
is due to not wanting to make mistakes. Whenever you are feeling
stuck, look around you and see the amazing things that have been
created because someone was willing to venture out in a new direction. They were willing to be flexible and adapt to change. For
example, magnificent mountains have been climbed by pioneer-
ing souls who were not afraid to take risks. Beautiful new vistas
and terrains were encountered. You can access a wealth of new
information and fascinating experiences by your willingness to
explore and be versatile.*

*Take a moment and bring to mind something that you have al-
ways wanted to do but have not yet accomplished. What are your
reasons for not taking the steps necessary to reach your goal? If it*

is due to thoughts of lack, begin by replacing limiting beliefs with thoughts of empowerment. Reach out and share your dream with those who would support you in your endeavors. You might find a like-minded group who has the same goal, and you can pool your resources together. Pray for assistance from the heavenly realms. Make a game plan and take a step each day that will lead you closer to your destination.

When I worked for a military organization on the earth plane, I was ordered to guard a storehouse of provisions. People passed by me every day, some in dire need of the foodstuffs that we had accumulated. They asked me to assist them in obtaining food. I was torn between obeying orders and helping those in need. One day, an officer passed by and gave me a large sack of grain. He said that I could give a cupful to townspeople who were hungry. I proceeded to do this until the bag was empty. However, I still needed to find a way to meet the large demand.

I didn't know how I could challenge the established protocol, but I prayed for an answer. It occurred to me that when I was a child I used to gather up seeds that were dropped by my father in the course of doing his work. After a while, I had a little stockpile of seeds and I turned them into a loaf of bread. I asked the commander if I could sweep up after the workers each day. He gave me permission and I found that I could accumulate quite a large sack of meal from the remnants left behind. I continued to distribute this food to the community.

I think that if we examine our lives, we can see areas where we have been stockpiling. There are probably areas where we have more than enough. I would encourage you to share the abundance.

If you have spiritual truths that you have gained, I am sure there are many others who would benefit by hearing them. Even if you feel inadequate, give what you have and the rest will be provided. Because you are willing to be an instrument of healing, you will be given support from the spiritual realms.

Can you imagine what the world would be like if nobody was afraid to change their current ways of behaving and thinking? Innovations would be taking place constantly, and there would be surpluses of everything. Extend yourself in a new way each day. If you are faced with obstacles, be versatile and try something different. Know that you are loved and supported by your Creator. He will assist you in every new endeavor that is for your highest good.

If something appears misaligned in your life, examine the reasons. I suggest that you reach inside of yourself to find answers and take action to change it. You have been sent here to be innovative, not complacent. Continue to rely on your inner strength and you will receive the sustenance you need. Share your spiritual truth, which is the bread of life. Evolve and grow, Jahallah.

I was driving my teenage daughter and her friend on an outing. The conversation turned to my work coordinating metaphysical events. Her friend blurted out, "Are you Christian or Catholic?" I listened intently because I was curious about how my daughter would respond. She thought about it for a moment and then brightly declared, "We're *versatile!*" I had to laugh out loud. "That's a good answer," I said. "I'll have to remember that one."

Over the past few years, I have been in conversations with fundamentalist thinkers who wonder if I am still following the "rules" that will lead to my salvation. Some people have expressed concern that I have strayed from the doctrines developed around Jesus Christ. Because I didn't feel the need to attack or defend, I usually said very little in response. Religious debate is not something that I indulge in.

The truth is that since I have been studying the *Course in Miracles* and other new thought principles, I have had a closer connection with Christ than ever before. As a child, I had a strong yearning to learn more about the teachings of Jesus. Because the *Course* was written for Jesus, I found a wealth of new information. Some old friends of mine have not been comfortable with exploring other paths to spirituality. I agree that the traditional texts are valuable resources for wisdom, but I think we are limiting ourselves if we don't explore the myriad ways to connect with our Creator.

When I began organizing programs, it was my intention to create spiritual gathering places where all paths to God were honored. As I have shared this work, I have become less reticent to discuss my beliefs and alternative spiritual practices. I am realizing that if I don't make the information easily available to people, it may be depriving them of venues for greater spiritual awareness and development. It doesn't feel authentic to withhold my truth just because they might think that I am odd. Once people explore other possibilities for themselves, they don't remain skeptical for long.

In my life, the study of metaphysics has brought me greater joy, peace, and connection with God. I use discernment when presented with any idea, whether it is old or new. To do this I go within myself for guidance and decide if it resonates with my personal truth. The bottom line is that no external authority has the formula that will create our relationship with the Divine. That answer is only found within.

I would encourage everyone to speak their truth without fear. I do not advocate evangelizing or arguing, just gentle sharing of alternative ways of being. As we examine the spiritual paths and traditions of all cultures, we create tolerance and understanding. The key to expansion is to remain versatile and open to change. In doing this, we find new solutions to problems and insights for our everyday lives. As we explore the infinite possibilities in our world, we will find the basic underlying universal truths that connect us all.

Angel of Versatility Prayer

"Mother-Father God, I seek wisdom and expanded awareness. I will be versatile and accept the many ways these gifts are offered to me. Challenges are overcome when I am flexible and allow the Universe to provide me with solutions. I ask for assistance from my spiritual helpers to lead me in the direction that will be best for the fulfillment of my life purpose. I acknowledge this assistance with humility and gratitude. And so it is."

Three ways that I will experience versatility in my life are:

1.

2.

3.

IDEAS:

1. Visit a new mosque, temple, church, or spiritual gathering.

2. Watch the movie *What the Bleep Do We Know!?*

3. Try a new way of communicating in a troubled relationship.

harmony

I would like to address the subject of harmony. It has been told to you that my presence is able to merge into your consciousness because of the harmonics or compatibility of our vibrations. This is true, and you will see other aspects of your life fall into place when it is your intention to create harmony.

As you go about your day, see the many ways that nature is effortlessly in harmony. There is a rhythm and flow to the existence of the plants, animals, and the elements. You can create harmony in your own life by understanding that humans can also practice the patterns of nature. If you feel "out of sorts," it may be due to energetic influences that can be cleared. In this earth plane, not everyone is in balance, and a multitude of energy exchanges take place that may not be beneficial. Blankets of energy can be lifted when you are in harmony with your Higher Source. Meditation and consciously running high-level energies through your body can remove external influences that are impeding the harmonic flow.

I would like to address the subject of harmony. Spirit communication is possible when two entities share their thought patterns. This happens because of the harmonics or compatibility of their vibrations. When you find yourself continuously needing to control or manipulate, this is an indicator that you are not in the flow. As you bring in Light, you will begin to notice a feeling of release. The path of least resistance will usually fit best into the overall scheme of things.

When I was on the earth plane, I had a meeting with a young girl who came to me for guidance. She was experiencing some pain in her family relationships. She knew that I could help her to raise her energy and this would help create harmony in her life. She began a daily practice of going within, meditating, and seeing the light of God in each person. The disharmony started to fall away because she had shifted her perceptions, beliefs, and energy field. This prompted her to take actions that were more loving, and a greater harmony resulted.

Procure a set of wind chimes and watch the way the winds toss the bells in different directions. They are coming together in a seemingly haphazard way, yet the result of this is a lovely, ever-changing melody. If you feel tossed about by the winds of fate, you might try to find the bits of harmony that are actually arising from the tempest.

Always remember that energy will follow your highest attention and intention. Harmony is created when you surrender to *the flow and do not resist it. There is a saying on earth that "what you resist, persists." You have also been taught that you can love what is, regardless of the external form.*

You only have two choices in each situation. You can choose the awareness of love or you can choose to perceive the blocks to love's presence. How do you feel when you choose the latter? You probably feel very unharmonious. Choose what you will, and it will not change God's love for you. However, remember that each action affects everyone else in Creation. Mankind is evolving in consciousness, and this may have triggered irrational behavior from those who are not ready to shift. Soon it will become easier to remove yourself from the drama and live in harmony. It is a goal that we are all working toward. Thank you for your participation in the symphony of life. Love and adoration, Jahallah.

It took me a while to write about this topic. I received an impression that it was supposed to be about my family, and I was waiting for my home life to become harmonious. Since I wanted to finish the book, I just sat down to write. I think that all of us are given our greatest opportunities for developing the thirty-three qualities I have been writing about by interacting with our own families. The people who are closest to us are our greatest teachers.

During my workday, I do my best to be sweet and helpful. However, on some evenings after a long day of spreading smiles and encouragement, I come home and I let my grumpy self out of the closet. I connected with this quote by Roseanne: "Women complain about premenstrual syndrome, but I think of it as the only time of the month that I can be myself." For the most part, this alter ego comes out when it is faced with dirty dishes and messy bedrooms.

I have the reputation for speaking my mind, sometimes very loudly. I am not one of those mothers who take on all of the household responsibilities and end up on prescription medications. Even though my kids might complain that I am not very domestic, I do believe that I have taught them self-sufficiency. To maintain harmony in a household, I think everyone needs to chip in and help out.

Sometimes I think the members of my family are like the wind chimes Jahallah mentioned. There may be more banging of heads than making music, but we are all doing our best. Even if we are going in opposite directions and have different values, we each have a unique contribution to make to the whole. My husband is very good at fixing things, and I have a knack for organization and multitasking. My kids are good at many things, so I am teaching them the fine arts of vacuuming, dusting, and grocery shopping.

It may sound like I am a slave driver, but I can't say my kids are really overworked. They have one morning and one afternoon chore to do. If they shirk their responsibilities, they need to complete additional chores. When my kids choose the two-chore option, it really reduces the disharmony between us. I have to say that my kids are pretty wonderful, for the most part. They do their schoolwork and stay out of trouble. They have good hearts and care about others.

They sometimes give me a hard time, but I am not always an angel, either. I believe it is my challenge in this lifetime to overcome anger and maintain my balance no matter what is going on around me. I think I am getting better at it, but I haven't become perfect yet. I know that instead of blaming my anger on other people's actions, I have to shift my attitudes and allow people to be who they are. I also allow them to pick up their own dirty socks.

On the morning that I wrote this chapter, I was feeling pretty pleased with myself. The house was in order, I had been consistent with discipline, and the kids had been fairly cooperative. I came home from work that night and asked, "Is the Universe taunting me?" I had left a list of two-minute chores for each person. When I walked in the door, I found my kitchen filled with ants. There were overflowing trash cans and messes all over the house. Nobody had helped out with the chores. I was incredulous, but I had yet another opportunity to practice what I preach.

Angel of Harmony Prayer

"Mother-Father God, I choose to be in harmony with your highest will for my life. I ask for encouragement and direction as I make decisions that will keep me in alignment with the Divine flow. May all of my relationships be healed and blocks to love's presence be removed. I am blessed to have the support of the angels who bring me light and joy. May all of my thoughts and actions be harmonious so that I might create heaven on earth. And so it is."

Three ways that I will experience harmony in my life are . . .

1.

2.

3.

IDEAS:

1. Practice clear communication in your interactions with others.

2. Attend a symphony and observe how the musicians blend their talents to create harmony.

3. Buy a set of wind chimes and watch the wind create a melody.

synchronicity

No one is where he is by accident and chance
plays no part in God's plan.

A COURSE IN MIRACLES

The subject for today's lesson is synchronicity. There is Divine order
in the universe. Your life is not a series of totally random occurrences. Fear sets in when people start to believe that the world
is unsafe and chaotic. Those images are perpetuated in the media
and mainstream culture. You are taught that, at any moment, you
might become the victim of a crime. There are no victims. On some
level, each person has agreed to experience each situation. That is
not to say that some, using their free will, act unlovingly and un-
justly. The balancing measure the Universe takes is that the energy
will be returned to them, and they will experience what they have
given out. Nothing is lost in creation, it only changes form.

I know that you remember a time when you felt as if an op-
pressive energy enveloped you. You were working through some
energy that you had accumulated from the past. You used spiritual

tools to bring yourself out of it and transmute the energy. Then one day, it lifted and you knew that it was over. When you repay old karma, you are free to create anew. Before coming to this planet, you designed a fascinating, complex plan of events to experience. There were certain people that you agreed to meet and work with. Many times you feel an instant rapport with new acquaintances. They may be members of your soul group.

Each person has an individual life mission, and soul groups work together for specific purposes as well. What is a soul group? It is a group of beings who dwell on a similar energy frequency and who spend lifetimes together as they learn and evolve. You have already met many who are in your soul group. Some people in your group have the intention to bring healing and spiritual wisdom to the planet. You are working together in these endeavors. When a group is gathered together, they help each other hold a vibration. That is why many people derive great benefit from group channeling or meditation circles.

Doesn't it give you a sense of comfort and support when synchronistic meetings take place? It is reassuring when the right person or information comes along when you need it. You have experienced so many of these events that you are not really surprised when they take place. You should expect them. As you open yourself up to synchronicity, you will experience more. Our Mother/Father Creator doesn't want you to feel adrift in an ocean of random occurrences. There is order and intelligence within all things. Synchronicities are your signposts along the way.

You might want to keep a journal, listing those little coincidences that take place each day. You will see that they add up quickly. They will reassure you that you are not alone and that you are receiving guidance and direction from all realms. Have you ever experienced meeting someone and feeling like you already knew them? That is a very big indicator that the person has a valuable message for you. Pay particular attention to song lyrics and book titles. They can sometimes be a way for your guides to bring you information.

I remember a time when I was striving to become a recognized musician. I sang songs about creating peace and wholeness. I was told that my chosen career would be difficult. However, I had a sense that I would be guided and assisted along the way because the message I was sharing was important. I had a strong connection with my spiritual helpers, and they would give me daily insights about how to proceed to make my dreams a reality. One day I met a man who was a promoter for the entertainment industry. He knew of a venue that would welcome my talents. We worked together and did very well. We made a powerful impact on many people's lives.

Ask for other synchronicities today. They are very fascinating and give you a boost. Remember to show appreciation to the Universe for everything that gives you direction and encouragement. Even minor interactions can create a shift of energy within you and give you inspiration. Some synchronicities will impact you in a manner that almost takes your breath away. Be aware of the reminders, large and small, that you are not alone, but guided by Divine wisdom. Peace be with you, Jahallah.

I attended a spirit communication session and was told that my husband Larry and I had karma to work through in this lifetime. In a past incarnation, we had lived in ancient Greece. I was a priestess in a temple and my husband was born to a family in my village. He had a clubbed foot and other birth defects. As was the custom during that time, his parents left him out in the wilderness to die of exposure because he was imperfect. I rescued him from this fate and found another family to take care of him. I made sure that he had money throughout his life, and he became a prominent member of the community despite his disabilities.

Larry has been saved from death during this lifetime as well. He was working on the elevator of a building built in 1929. He was on a ladder, pulling new wire into the hoistway. The building had a bad ground and it shorted to the elevator rails. When he grabbed the rails to balance himself, he was electrocuted. His heart stopped, and he could see his skeleton as his spirit moved out of his body. He fell nine stories down the hoistway, hitting cables and brackets on the way down. Miraculously, he hit the ground and his heart started again. He got up and drove himself to the hospital, where the doctors and other onlookers gathered around to see how he had survived.

There were other times he had tempted fate and lived to tell about it. When he was in his twenties, he and his friends were riding motorcycles down a canyon road. He was going about one hundred miles an hour. As he turned a corner, he did a two-wheel drift and sideswiped a car. The bike slid on its side, narrowly avoiding the side of the cliff. The bike seemed to bounce back up of its own volition. Then as he approached the mountain on the other side, his bike went down again and popped back up. He must have had guardian angels working overtime during that episode. He pulled over and shook for about two hours.

The synchronistic thing about all this is that he has had several opportunities to save other people's lives. When he was eighteen years old, he joined the army. His platoon was assigned to move six-hundred-pound pipes. Some people lost their balance, and one recruit fell underneath a pipe. It crushed his throat and he could not breathe. Larry took out a pocketknife and a pen. He slit a hole in the cap of the pen and in the man's neck. He inserted the cap and fashioned an airway that he could breathe through until the paramedics arrived.

Another incident occurred on vacation at the Colorado River. A little boy was diving off the dock, and the current dragged him up underneath a floating cocktail bar. The boy's father was frozen in shock and unable to go after him. Larry jumped in and found the child stuck in the cables that anchored the platform. He pulled the unconscious body out of the water and began CPR and mouth-to-mouth resuscitation. The boy sputtered up water and began to cry. He and his parents were overwhelmed with gratitude.

More recently, Larry was on a street corner in the city waiting to cross at the light. A mother pushing a baby stroller approached with her four-year-old daughter on a bicycle. The little girl headed into the intersection and the light had not turned green. A car was speeding toward her and Larry stepped forward and pulled the girl off the bike by the scruff of the neck. The car actually skimmed Larry's body and the mirror hit him and broke off. The car never stopped, totally destroying the bicycle. The little girl was uninjured.

It seems that my husband has the knack for being at the right place at the right time and knowing what to do in an emergency. Saving three lives is probably against the odds of probability. It is amazing to think about these situations that necessitated split-second timing and action. As you evaluate your own life, I'm sure you will start to see how the cosmic game plan is playing out. Even less dramatic encounters and synchronicities have significance. I hope the fact that you are reading this book will have a positive impact on your journey.

Angel of Synchronicity Prayer

"Mother-Father God, thank you for the many ways you provide support and guidance in my life. I am certain that a Divine plan for my life is unfolding and that I am safe and supported. I will recognize the gifts of each holy encounter. I express gratitude for the amazing lightworkers that cross my path. May we continue to create healing and growth on this planet. Please give me direction so that I experience a life filled with ease, love, and abundance. And so it is."

Three ways that I will experience synchronicity in my life are . . .

1.

2.

3.

IDEAS:

1. Write down coincidences in a notebook to read at a later time and notice how events fell into place to create positive change.

2. Perform a random act of kindness anonymously to impact someone's life at the moment they need help.

3. Go to a social gathering with the intention of meeting someone special.

accomplishment

It doesn't matter what we do until we accept ourselves. Once we accept ourselves, it doesn't matter
what we do.

CHARLY HEAVENRICH

*Dear one, I am here to speak with you about accomplishment
and ambition. We see many people in the world striving to accomplish things. Their focus is usually on material possessions,
but there is much more in life that will bring fulfillment. Imagine
that you are in a place with no objects. What would your ambitions be then? Would they be to create peace within? Would you
like to create joy that is not contingent on outside circumstances?*

*Please be honest with yourself for a moment. What motivates
your daily activities? Is it a need for approval from others? That is
a very transitory thing indeed. People's opinions change with the
wind. Do you work toward goals because of a need to be accepted
or fit in? If so, you might want to reexamine why you are trying to
conform to this mold. What is intrinsically valuable in the status*

quo? Evolution takes place more quickly when you reach beyond the boundaries that have already been established.

I am not discounting the marvels that man, through his God self, has created. There is much to enjoy and appreciate on this planet. I am just reminding you that in other realms, material things do not play such an important role. It will be easier for you to make transitions in awareness if you don't have strong attachments to them. Some spirits become earthbound because of their strong bond with the physical realm. Some have the belief that substances, such as drugs or alcohol, are their means of salvation. By salvation, I mean a method of being released from fear and pain. We can see that these coping mechanisms can only have short-term success. They will not accomplish ultimate freedom and release. The practice of nonattachment will bring you closer to that goal.

Life is not a mystery that needs to be figured out. It is a passion play, and you are writing the script. Some of you have decided to play the role of the deal maker, creating money and power. These ambitions will prove very exhausting after a while. It takes a lot of energy to maintain physical manifestations, whereas things of the Spirit are readily available to you at all times. For example, if you desire peace, it is yours in an instant. If you choose joy, you will feel joyful. When your foremost goal is connection with the God force, your burdens will be light and your paths made easy.

Take an inventory of things in your life that are exhausting you. Are they really necessary to maintain your well-being, or are they designed to keep you busy? Scientists have found that preoccupation with material success can create stress and physical maladies. As you maintain a balance of focus, you will create balance in your body. Beliefs and emotions have a powerful impact on your physical experience. For example, your society has quite an aversion to the feeling of boredom. Understandably so, because it is an ego-created phenomenon. It is possible, however, to be absolutely still, do nothing, and not be bored.

If you want to try this, I suggest that you retreat into a quiet spot in nature to practice. If you are surrounded by impatient people who also have a fear of boredom, it may be difficult to raise your vibrations. Feelings are contagious, unless you are able to maintain your personal energy field and connection with your Source of peace. Your goal is to reconnect with that part of yourself that is infinite and limitless, unlike the fleeting world of illusion. You will become more proficient at this with practice. In the meantime, you can ask your guides and angels to create a protective shield that blocks out unwanted energies.

During one of my lifetimes, I wanted to find a way to become famous. I practiced yogic arts until I became adept at performing miraculous feats. Crowds would gather to witness the spectacle and toss coins into my jar. There was a holy man who passed by my camp. He was very unassuming, yet his energy soothed and healed people. He counseled them and offered them spiritual wisdom. He did not have much material wealth to show for his talents, but he seemed to glow with light and contentment.

One day I was counting my money and unwinding from an eventful demonstration. I was given much adulation and praise, but when the people left I felt somehow empty and let down. I sought out the holy man and asked him the secret to peace of mind. He said that my intentions would need to be changed in order to receive *more heavenly gifts. The tricks that I performed were meaningless unless they taught spiritual lessons. He encouraged me to be more concerned with being of service than with being admired.*

As you walked through the carnival today, you saw a game called "Treasure Chase." This was a reflection of the goals and ambitions of your society. If there is a buried treasure, it is the one you can find deep within yourself. Go there now and see if you can find it. This will be a very worthwhile accomplishment. Much love and support, Jahallah.

There are times in your life when you ask yourself, "What have I accomplished?" When I turned forty years old, I went through a mini midlife crisis. It only lasted about four days and then I snapped out of it. I was measuring my success by worldly standards and found myself not measuring up. The fact that I was not independently wealthy was making me feel like a failure. Friends and family helped me to recognize the contributions and accomplishments that I have made during my lifetime. I can look back and see that I have touched many people's lives to give them love and encouragement.

I didn't know what to write in this chapter, so I asked family and friends to fill out a questionnaire to gain an understanding of what people consider valuable accomplishments. I spent a lot of time and energy on this project, but didn't come up with any conclusive answers. There was no consensus on what was important and what was not. I did realize, however, that we are each an irreplaceable part of the whole and God's creation is incomplete without us. The fact that we agreed to incarnate here for our own soul growth is a substantial accomplishment.

I have heard that other places in the Universe are less dense and chaotic than earth, but the challenges we face here help us to evolve more quickly. My husband chose a very dysfunctional and painful childhood, but those experiences fast-forwarded him to another level of consciousness. He was able to overcome obstacles instead of becoming mired in them. He feels that providing a stable, supportive home for our three children is his greatest accomplishment. I must agree that the kids have turned out well, even though I'm not sure how we did it. We fulfilled our commitment to staying together as a family for close to twenty years.

My oldest son, Anthony, has probably worked hard in past lifetimes and many things come easily to him now. He is very industrious, has a sharp mind and is able to master many tasks. I am impressed when I see him recognize his inner power. We bought a trampoline, and he taught himself to do a backflip one afternoon. He said, "I just tell myself I can do something, and I can." I'm sure we all can recall incidents when our confidence and power created success in our lives. The real trick is remembering to do that on a daily basis.

My youngest son Christopher can also accomplish similar feats through sheer determination. He is a warrior with a lot of energy, and he usually gets what he wants. The world needs warriors to change the existing status quo if it is not working. He is a talented athlete and has a room filled with trophies to show for it. He feels that his greatest accomplishment is maintaining the skill and discipline necessary to excel in his chosen sports. I know he will do well in whatever he chooses to accomplish in life as he keeps his single-minded focus.

My daughter, Briana, is an easygoing person who has a very compassionate heart. She wants to become a veterinarian. She tends to her horse, rabbits, dog, birds and other animals with great maternal instincts. She has excelled in her animal husbandry education and extracurricular programs. She does well because she uses her natural abilities to pursue the activities that bring her joy.

My family taught me that love, belief, determination and pursuing our passions will create accomplishment. I tried the route of the perfectionist, but that never got me very far. I worked hard and fully expected to see magnificent results from every endeavor. Living this way created frustration and burnout. Through the process of writing this book, I stopped being so hard on myself. I put my heart and soul into the project, but I let the Universe handle the outcome. I knew that even if I didn't see all the trappings of worldly success around me, I had made great strides on my spiritual path.

Life is all about creating balance and following your guidance in each moment. I read a quote by Bob Dylan that said, "A man is a success if he gets up in the morning, goes to bed at night, and in between he does what he wants to do." By those standards, I am pretty successful after all.

Angel of Accomplishment Prayer

"Mother-Father God, I ask that you direct me in finding my way back to You. In doing this, all support is
available to me to make my dreams a reality. I will
create abundance in many ways, without stress or
strain. I will be an instrument of peace and healing
in my world. I know that as I look within, I will find
valuable gifts to share with others. I can accomplish
great things through my God Self. Speak to me each
day, that I may be of service to You. And so it is."

Three things I will do to experience accomplishment are . . .

1.

2.

3.

IDEAS:

1. Set three small goals that can be accomplished in a week
   and use joy, inner empowerment, and determination to
   achieve them.

2. Treat yourself to dinner at a fine restaurant to celebrate
   an accomplishment, even if it took place years ago.

3. Design a ritual prayer invoking and thanking spiritual
   leaders for their contributions to the world.

prosperity

If you refuse to accept anything but the best, you'll
get the best. Begin to live as you wish to live.

UNKNOWN

*Today's lesson is about prosperity. You have been focusing on this
subject a lot over the last year. You have been using many tools
and doing inner work to clear blocks. One block people encounter
is in their openness to receive. You may think, "I am ready," but
lingering beliefs in lack may still be haunting you. We were all
given messages about money during our upbringing. Some of them
were positive and many were not. Do you believe that you are
worthy to receive great things? If so, they shall be given unto you.*

*Everything is activated by exchanges of energy. Good fortune is
generated when you are willing to give and receive. Before you go
any further, please stop to assess the ways that you give to others
in your life. Also, take a look at the many things you receive. Some
people who perceive themselves as poor may really have a wealth
of resources at their disposal. One needs to make use of what has*

been given. You each have many talents and abilities that you can contribute to the world. Your efforts will be repaid. That is universal law.

Prosperity means to have an abundance of good things. A writer in the Bible rejoiced that his cup was running over. This is the natural state of affairs when you are aligned with Spirit. There is more than enough for everyone. Just remember, in order for your cup to be filled, you must empty it of anything that is stopping the flow.

This might be thoughts, feelings, actions, or beliefs that are limiting. Please take a moment to go within now and think of any area of your life that is out of alignment with your highest integrity and purpose. It is not difficult for most people to see what parts of their lives are not working. They probably even know what to do to fix them, but hesitate to take action. If you are at a loss for what direction to take, ask your angels and guides for assistance. Don't rely on them, however, to do the work for you. Open yourself up and let God do his work through you. All it takes is a little willingness. You will be met halfway by Spirit. Openness is the key. Be open to change. Be open to love. Be open to your highest knowing.

Prosperity will manifest in your life when there is agreement on all levels of your being—emotional, mental, and spiritual. Angels are spiritual beings who express their authentic selves and are filled with great joy. They don't have worries about how their needs will be met. Their focus is on extending themselves to us and helping us to remember who we truly are. They play music and enjoy sharing their energy with others.

During one lifetime, I was a tambourine player for a traveling minstrel show. My partners and I didn't make a lot of money and relied on the donations of our audiences. One day we visited the palace of a wealthy aristocrat. He was a stern gentleman who was used to getting what he wanted. He decided that he liked our music and wanted us to stay on as his personal musicians. He would pay us large sums of money to be on call at his residence. We all felt that the joy and adventure would be gone from our lives if we agreed to this. We opted to continue touring around the country. When we followed our hearts, we became well known and made a profitable living.

Expand your idea of how money can be created. As consciousness shifts on this planet, people will be seeking assistance outside of the established economic channels. Alternative healthcare and counseling services will be in demand as people search for the best ways to heal their mind, bodies, and spirits. Money is one means of exchange on this planet, but not the only one. Prosperity takes on many forms. Loving family, supportive friends, good health, and right livelihood are all things that add abundance to our lives. I want to give a note of encouragement to those who feel they don't have any of those things. Karma may be a factor that influences your present level of prosperity, but don't let that discourage you. Let it motivate you to work through the energy of the past and move forward. There is no limit to what you can create with your God self.

Yes, it can be discouraging when many areas of your life are not working. Be assured that great growth is taking place because you have chosen this path. Remember, however, that these problems are things to move through. Don't linger along the wayside, immersing yourself in their energy. Keep your energy levels high *and try not to get weighed down by depression or frustration. True prosperity will be gained when you surmount these obstacles. The gratitude you will feel after the process is finished will be great. You will have a greater appreciation for life when your way becomes smooth again. Gratitude is another key to keeping the flow of prosperity going in your life. Like attracts like. If you receive and you are grateful, you will receive more.*

If you find yourself obsessing about money, take a step back and reevaluate where you are putting most of your energy. Nature thrives on balance. We don't expect you to have every mystery of the universe solved. The excitement comes from the journey to find the answers. If this quest prevents you from feeling at peace, then stop immediately. Nothing is worth giving up the birthright of your true self. Make it a game, and don't take it so seriously.

Many have played the game and succeeded. They have written books about how you can create prosperity like they did. Use the information that is useful to you, but their path is not your path. Only you can determine the best way to gain prosperity. Don't underestimate your power to know and tap into the universal intelligence. You are just as well equipped to succeed as anyone else. The final key is that you already have everything, now. Accept it. Joy and blessings, Jahallah.

I have to admit that this chapter was a bit more challenging for me to write than the others. For years, I did a lot of work on my prosperity consciousness. Just when I thought I was making progress, I ended up taking a few steps back. I became involved in some ventures designed to bring in wealth, but I ended up losing money.

Since I didn't think I was an authority on this subject, I asked several wealthy colleagues to write about their insights, but nobody responded. (I guess they were too busy earning more money.) I even coordinated a prosperity workshop, hoping to have a life-changing experience. I did, in a way. The person teaching the class cancelled the day before the event because she wanted more money. She also refused to reimburse me for the many hours of computer work that I had done on her workshop materials.

That was the final kick in the butt that made me realize nobody had answers exactly right for me. I had to figure out ways to bring in my own abundance. I think that Spirit wanted me to write this chapter in order to "move energy" on this issue. Each day I would look at ways to build my career and take steps toward achieving my short- and long-term goals. I prayed and meditated as well. I reminded myself not to be attached to outcomes and to be grateful for each step forward. I believe that our inner life is reflected in our outer world, so I paid attention to how my life unfolded each day. I tried not to make superficial judgments, such as "success" or "failure," but noticed how each incident influenced my growth.

Two books about prosperity that I recommend are *Creating Money* by Sanaya Roman and *Creating True Prosperity* by Shakti Gawain. Shakti wrote that "prosperity is the experience of having plenty of what we truly need and want in life—material and otherwise." She pointed out that new age teachings about manifesting money can leave people frustrated. If they say all the "right" affirmations and believe they are open to receive, it can be depressing if the wealth doesn't appear. We start to wonder what is wrong with us and what we are doing wrong.

It is not always productive to judge external circumstances, because each person's path is unique. Just because they are not rich, it does not mean they have failed. When we choose to incarnate on this planet, sometimes we choose to be royalty, a celebrity, or a wealthy entrepreneur, and sometimes we choose to be a schoolteacher, a housewife, or a social worker. Each path is perfect for that lifetime and has its own rewards and lessons to teach us.

Money is not the final determinant of prosperity because people on all income levels feel like they don't have enough. What I think is invaluable is the peaceful feeling of security that can be achieved by surrendering our lives to Spirit. We all have the choice to see the glass as half full or half empty. I admit that there have been days when I panicked a bit after not receiving what I thought were my "just rewards." One week I thought that I had a wonderful life, and the next week I was worried that I had made all the wrong choices. It was the same life situation, the only thing that had changed was my perception of it.

Shakti wrote, "True prosperity is not something we create overnight. In fact, it is not a fixed goal, a place where we will finally arrive, or a certain state that we will someday achieve. It is an ongoing process of finding fulfillment that continues to unfold and deepen throughout our lives." I have spent several years establishing the groundwork for the career that I would like in writing, healing, networking, and counseling. I believe that the effort I put into these endeavors will pay off financially, but I will try not to lose my focus about why I am doing them.

As I continue to make spiritual growth my first priority, I know the details about my finances will fall into place. As I take topics from this book and "work them," I know that it will clear my energetic channels and I will receive wealth. For example, as I create flowing energy in the areas of trust, gratitude, following my joy, healing my wounds, giving to others, releasing fear, and participating in the dance of life, I will find myself receiving more abundance. When I look back, I can see how the Universe has always provided for me each step along this journey. Because I am filled with peace and well-being in the present moment, I am sure that the future will be filled with even more joy and prosperity.

Angel of Prosperity Prayer

"Mother-Father God, I pray that you will assist me
in releasing all fear and thoughts of lack. I know that
great growth and spiritual healing will take place as
a result of the work I do on the planet. I ask to be
well-supported financially, spiritually, emotionally,
and physically. Please help me to let go of money concerns so that I can better enjoy the present. I am open

to receive all of the prosperity and blessings of the Universe, now. And so it is."

Three ways that I will experience prosperity in my life are . . .

1.

2.

3.

IDEAS:

1. Read *Excuse Me, Your Life Is Waiting,* and after opening up your energy valves, embark on a new business venture.

2. Learn abundance principles from spiritually based books and pass the information on to someone else.

3. Every time a money concern arises, shift your attention to a positive resolution or an existing blessing.

synergy

There is no more sure tie between friends than
when they are united in their objects and wishes.

CICERO

Individually, we are each powerful beings. However, when we com-bine our energies, it amplifies our ability to create. It is a rare gift to find a group of spirits with a blend of abilities and talents that complement one another. As long as everyone has the same intent, it is easy to successfully make dreams a reality together.

Spirit communication is a means to connect once again and participate in a cooperative undertaking. This creates synergy. When we work together, a greater impact is made in manifesta-tion. You and I have common goals. One is to impress upon people the importance of working together. What you do to another, you do to yourself. We all are derived from the same Source. As we ex-plored the multitudes of possibilities of experience, different arche-types and patterns arose. However, on the deepest level, we re-mained connected.

On earth, you have created many boundaries, separating yourselves from one another. Your minds are no longer strongly connected unless you revive your innate abilities, such as telepathy. In addition to closing down your spiritual connection, you put fences around your homes and lock up all of your possessions. Great amounts of money are spent on protecting what is "yours" in the form of high-tech alarm systems and security devices. What you are forgetting is that we are all One. As we reawaken our remembrance of this fact, the need to attack, defend, or protect diminishes.

Periodically in your life you will come across an event that reminds you that what you give, you receive. You feel your heart fill with joy when you help someone in need, without regard for repayment. This is because you are giving to yourself. On the other hand, when you hold on to things and hoard them, it creates an emotion that is not as pleasant. That is because you are withholding from yourself.

When I was a child in a past incarnation, my mother was concerned about providing enough food for her family. There was one man in the village who had money and access to supplies. Most of the villagers became indebted to him over time. Hard feelings started to develop as people were unable to repay their debts. The sense of community was lost as competition for survival arose. One day my mother called a meeting of the village women. She asked them to send light to this man and pray for the softening of hearts.

She took a collection of any goods that the families could spare. She brought them to the lender as payment for the collective debt. The man received the gifts graciously and asked her to eat with him. She was unaccustomed to being in a home of such *grandeur, but she accepted the invitation. Moments later, there was a knock on the door. It was a young boy from a neighboring village who had lost his way. He was brought inside to share in the meal.*

Some of the servants became disgruntled, because they wondered if there would be enough food left for them. The master of the house said that there would be no one who would go without sustenance on that evening. He made sure that everyone in the village was contacted and given what they needed for the night. His storehouses of goods seemed to diminish, but this did not cause alarm. The energy of generosity and support spread and each member of the village was touched and transformed. They agreed to take one day at a time and try to supply everyone's needs. They accomplished their goal each day by working together.

Our Creator wants each one of us to partake of the banquet that is available. Holy is the moment when two or more come together for good. The synergy created in this joining amplifies the light that spreads throughout the universe. Part of your mission in this life is to cooperate and live in harmony with those around you. This is a gift and blessing to those who experience it. Go out into your world and see what synergistic connections arise in your daily life. Honor each encounter and know that all the power of Creation is behind you. May your blessings be manifold, Jahallah.

For a few years, I coordinated spiritual renewal festivals. After a while, I ran out of steam because I was working extremely hard. I sought assistance from others and found that the most successful events were created by a team effort. Various partners would chip in to handle different aspects of the program coordination.

I met many talented people over the years. Some of those practitioners would later join me in the Spiritual Awareness Network of Southern California. At the onset of these projects, I really had no intention of networking. Making connections came naturally to me. I would be guided to make introductions and connections for people. I would assist others in promoting their work, and my efforts were recognized and appreciated.

My Web site took form as though it was divinely organized. Even the name, www.spiritualawarenessnetwork.org, was created by chance. The other domains that we wanted were taken, but when we added the word "network," it seemed right. This dynamic reminded me of a quote by Henry Miller: "The world is not to be put in order; the world is order incarnate. It is for us to harmonize with this order."

My spirit guides are very active in my work. My "noodging" angels are always giving me strong guidance to help and support others in the metaphysical community. Sometimes, it feels as though I need to assist people in order to maintain my peace. As we join together in a group, we create a synergy that would be impossible to achieve alone. Synergy is "combined action in which the total effect is greater than the sum of the effects taken independently."

I found this dynamic in action at a marketing workshop that I attended. I asked a new member of the spiritual network, Lisa Cherney, to come and share her expertise with us. She had experience with Fortune 500 companies and also used her intuition to help people discover powerful ways to spread their message. I had heard positive recommendations from my colleagues, and I was eager to see what all the excitement was about. Many of my friends were lightworkers and were interested in new ways to expose their work to more people.

We brainstormed for ways to advertise the unique products and services that we had to offer. We worked with a packet of worksheets that approached marketing sideways. Instead of struggling with creating taglines, etc., we did visualizations and exercises to explore our passions and talents. We teamed up and supported each other in our visions. We were encouraged not to use our logical minds to determine outcomes, but to set our energies and intentions at a high level. In this manner, we would use the law of attraction to bring about our desired results.

We were asked to create a virtual "Board of Directors" to motivate us. The board is made up of mentors in various areas (i.e., finances, marketing, spirituality, etc.) and we honor them with the request to support our vision. As I developed my "dream team" of advisors, I realized that many of the people in my daily life were my inspirations. Famous people such as Oprah Winfrey and Eckhart Tolle made my list, but so did dear friends and acquaintances who have inspired me to reach higher.

We were reminded that we are not alone. Spirit guides help us each day and many other beings are available as well if we just ask. Sometimes I feel like a little helper is whispering in my ear. I receive reminders about commitments and ideas for completing tasks efficiently. Obviously, I was given a lot of guidance in the process of writing this book. I had renewed appreciation for the assistance of my guide Jahallah and the angels whose energy prompted me to move forward.

Another exercise that we did during this workshop was to start a sentence with "My heart is telling me . . ." and complete it over and over again, letting our stream of consciousness guide us. It was amazing how the intention of reaching deep and accessing what we really wanted had such a profound affect. We uncovered hopes, dreams, pain, fears, joy, and power. This self-exploration and excavation helped us to uncover some significant issues. Sometimes, as we get busy in our daily lives, we forget what really is important to us. If we do these types of exercises regularly, our higher self will keep us focused on the most rewarding path.

The benefits of synergy were immediately apparent after this workshop. I was given encouragement and insights for promoting my book. Another person was starting a dating service for spiritually minded singles and found a venue to share her work with hundreds of people that night. We gained renewed enthusiasm for reaching people and sharing many opportunities for growth and healing at this gathering.

Many look at the apparent chaos on our planet and think that things will never get better. I have a more optimistic outlook about the future because I am connecting with loving, kind people every day. My worldview does not match the one portrayed by the television media. I am looking forward to the day when everyone will embrace the gifts awaiting them by connecting with the Divine. I think the tide will change as more of us come together to share the light and connect with the spirits that are also working with us to create this paradigm shift. I give thanks daily for the assistance I receive from my earth angels and my heavenly helpers.

Angel of Synergy Prayer

"Mother-Father God, I am part of you and you are part of me. It is in union with my Source that I find my peace, my power, my joy, and all manner of blessings. I appreciate the diversity life contains and the synergistic unions that take place in my life. I know that I am supported by my brothers and sisters on earth and in the spiritual realms. I take advantage of opportunities to give as well as to receive. As we join together, we make great strides toward raising the universal consciousness. And so it is."

Three things I will do to create synergy in my life are . . .

1.

2.

3.

IDEAS:

1. Join a *Course in Miracles* study group to gain the assistance of others in implementing the principles into your daily life.

2. Seek out a huge meditation gathering and feel the vibrant energy created by the event. Send the energy out into the world to create healing.

3. Become a member of a noncompetitive networking group and assist others in achieving their business goals.

understanding

The meaning of things lies not in the things themselves, but in our attitude towards them.

ANTOINE DE SAINT EXUPERY

Why me? Why this? Why now? All around you people are lament-
ing about their troublesome lives. They have no idea why they
have been dealt such burdens. With understanding, they will find
release. Psychics who have a strong connection with the spiritual
realms may be able to access some answers. However, everyone
has the ability to use their own intuition to solve their problems.

When I was on the earth plane, I had an experience that cre-
ated quite a shock. I approached a stranger on the street to ask for
directions. He was extremely rude, and I didn't understand what I
had done to be treated in such a manner. I returned home and de-
scribed him to my brother. It turns out that he was the friend of a
gentleman who did business with my family. There had been some
sort of dispute in a financial transaction.

I didn't understand why I had been dragged into this because I had not been a participant in the disagreement. I actually became very angry and was going to seek out the man for another confrontation. A wise woman in the village advised me that this gentleman and I had a quarrel in a previous lifetime. He immediately looked upon me with suspicion and mistrust. He was given an opportunity to act upon this energy and did so. She felt that if I retaliated, the cycle would continue. It was best to send the stranger loving energy and pray for a shift of consciousness to take place.

A week later, I saw the man in the street again. I walked to the other side of the road to avoid him. He pursued me and insisted that we talk. He said that he wanted to apologize for his behavior. He asked me to join him for a meal in the marketplace. I resisted for a moment because I had not released all of my anger. Then my higher self regained more presence and I knew that I would only harm myself if I perpetuated the negativity. I can't say that we became fast friends, but he did do me a kind favor later in life. I felt that we no longer had karma to resolve with each other.

You can take every circumstance in your life and ask your higher guidance for the lesson it contains. Once you break a pattern or have an attitude of forgiveness or acceptance, the problems will melt away. Your soul has designed certain scenarios in your life in order to grow and evolve. Because you do not have the entire picture in your waking state, it is best not to judge things as "bad" or "good." Instead, remain in the present moment and act from a place of love and understanding. Become a detached observer if you can. You will find that emotions such as fear and anger will arise less frequently when you do this.

Transformation occurs when many different forces come to-gether to impact a person. Picture the ironworker who forges steel with fire. He fabricates useful tools by impacting the metal with various elements and uses of resistance. There is no remorse that the original substance must go through extreme duress in order to change form. It is part of a plan to create something new and more beneficial.

Yes, dear one, you sometimes feel that you are being run through the mill. Have courage, for when you persevere, you will find the end result very valuable indeed. Fate is not something to fear. Be as-sured that your higher intelligence is guiding you on a journey that will lead you back to a state of perfection. All you can do in the meantime is to refrain from immersing yourself in resistance, bitter-ness, or feelings of impotence. There is a reason that you are here now. Blessings on your road to self-discovery, Jahallah.

One year, I had dreams about my teenage son Anthony. I sensed that he was going to make choices that would result in harmful consequences. I was hosting an ongoing psychic de-velopment class at the time, and I asked the teacher what his insights were in the situation. He picked up on an accident my older son might have on an off-road vehicle. This was not very encouraging information, but I knew my son was in charge of his own life. At sixteen years of age, he was motor-cycle riding every weekend. He was doing well in school and had a part-time job. He had just gotten his driver's license and purchased his first truck.

Two days later, I received a call that my son was being taken to the hospital. He had crashed his motorcycle and dislocated his shoulder. I wasn't too upset because we had gone through that before. I used to joke that the emergency room staff knew us on a first-name basis. We made my son comfortable when he got home, and I thought it would be business as usual. The worst-case scenario was that he would be out of physical education at school and would undergo a few months of physical therapy.

I had a psychic reading the next day with my friend Anarah. She had been a family counselor for us over the years. She looked at the situation energetically and saw a past life "lighting up." She said that my son had been a member of a sailing crew that pillaged a town. Many crimes were committed, and three people were hung. My son was one of them. Although he was not a ringleader, he was one of the "fall guys." Anarah said, "Amy, I am worried about his neck. It was very vulnerable due to this past experience and I think he may have an injury." I told her that the doctors had not seen a problem.

When I returned home, there was a phone message on my machine indicating that the x-ray technicians had found a fracture on Anthony's fifth vertebrae. I was stunned, but not really surprised. The way this had unfolded, I had an understanding of the reasons things were happening. We took him back to the hospital where he was outfitted with a neck brace. We had a rough night, but I think my hysteria was held in check due to the information I had received psychically.

It was a difficult situation for everyone, and my son was on his back for a long time. We had a teacher come to our home with his schoolwork. I bought Anthony *The Power of Now* by Eckhart Tolle on audiotape. I hoped it would inspire him to look past his current life situation and look within for peace and comfort. I think it helped him to see life from another perspective, and he learned valuable lessons through this challenging experience. We talked about making wise decisions in regard to friends and peer situations and going within for guidance. Sometimes it is hard to accept the cards we are dealt in life, but there is a bigger picture designed to help us evolve and gain greater understanding of ourselves. With greater understanding, acceptance becomes easier. As we practice acceptance, we will find peace.

Angel of Understanding Prayer

"Mother-Father God, I believe there is a reason for each event in my life. This gives me strength and courage to continue growing and evolving. My soul has designed lessons that I will utilize to gain wisdom and understanding. I will refrain from judging situations as "good" or "bad," but view them from many perspectives. I ask for guidance and insights along the way to keep me in touch with Truth. When I find the Truth, it will set me free. And so it is."

Three ways that I will experience understanding in my life
are . . .

1.

2.

3.

IDEAS:

1. Look back on your life and realize how a seeming "crisis" helped to heal everyone involved.

2. Generate respect for someone you disagree with and attempt to view the argument from another perspective.

3. Learn and practice a new spiritual discipline in order to
   more deeply understand universal laws.

destiny

We are as but the instrument of heaven. Our work
is not design, but destiny.

LORD LYTTON

I would like to speak to you today about choosing your destiny.
Please do not settle for less than you are capable of becoming. You
are a being of infinite potential and scope. You are entering a time
when a dimensional shift is taking place. You signed up to be a
part of this experience. It is your destiny to be a way-shower and
pioneer. Everyone alive on this planet today will play a role in the
dramatic changes occurring in the earth's consciousness.

We will be moving from a three-dimensional universe to a
four-dimensional one. This means that you will need to shed old
belief systems and limitations. Because you are preparing for
these changes by expanding your awareness, the shifts will come
more easily. Accessing Christ consciousness is a way to interface
with a higher vibration.

When the Master Jesus was on your planet, he helped people to shed limitations by raising their vibratory level. This created a way to transform matter into antimatter. This means that you can cast aside worries about lack because your ability to manifest will be unlimited.

During one incarnation, I was given the responsibility of gathering souls together for an instructional seminar. The purpose of the meeting was to compare notes on global problems and brainstorm for solutions. There were many things to do. I had to make contacts and create a large gathering of lightworkers. For the most part, people were cooperative. However, they were going in so many different directions that it took a lot of energy to pull them together. I found myself becoming very preoccupied and serious.

A traveling circus was passing through town at the time. The streets were crowded with people trying to reach their destinations. An entertainer stopped me in the street and asked me if I could show him the way to the gathering place. I assumed that he was looking for our lightworker symposium, so I pointed out the courtyard where we were meeting. When he arrived, he saw people immersed in intense, serious conversations. He thought that a circus crowd would have been more lighthearted. He reached into his travel case and pulled out some props to perform tricks.

He had the people chuckling and forgetting for a moment about the weighty problems that they were trying to solve. Their laughter increased, as did the vibration of their energy fields. When it was finally time to "get down to work," they were better prepared to access information from their higher selves without stress or resistance. They had important work to do, but the opportunity to relax and enjoy life was also appropriate.

Your destiny is something that has been preordained. You do have freedom of choice, but when you choose in opposition to your destiny, your life becomes a struggle. You are a source of light and healing to others. If you would like to discover your own destiny, follow these simple guidelines. Go within and ask the questions, "Who am I? Why am I here?" Start writing in a stream of consciousness manner. Don't worry if your words do not make sense at first. You will filter out the message that you are to receive.

Everyone has a unique role to fulfill in this world. Each job is equally valuable. Your mission will be something that you are good at and that comes easily to you. You may be here to help people laugh or you may be here to help people think. You are all here to help each other to love. Don't miss an opportunity to fulfill your destiny. You will receive many rewards when you are on your path. You have my gratitude for all of your efforts, Jahallah.

Through my networking endeavors, I met people who provided me with opportunities for sharing my truth. A lovely woman named Suzan was hosting a monthly nondenominational service called Illuminations 22 at the Learning Light in Anaheim, California. They conducted free healings and billet readings and featured guest speakers and musicians each month. Even though I don't really enjoy public speaking, Suzan encouraged me to stretch myself. This opportunity gave me a chance to talk about the things that have had a big influence on my life, such as peace, spiritual service, and Christ force energy.

As I talked, I acknowledged the efforts everyone had made to be on their path in order to raise the consciousness of the planet. I felt that it was no accident that we were gathered together. I wanted to encourage each of them to look within and find the gifts they had that would help the world to heal. If they lacked confidence or were unsure of how to proceed, their true self or Christ self would guide them. When I went within to find my purpose, I received a loud answer: "You will help people create a stronger connection to their Christ selves."

Christ consciousness unites us with God and with one another. Our Christ selves have not lost connection with the Creator. It maintains the innocence in which it was created. When we remember our true selves, there will be no more separation or illusion. The pain that we have created will fade when we remember the truth of who we are.

I may have a strong connection with this energy because of my past life during the time Jesus was on the planet. Various psychics would relate stories to me about that lifetime. I wanted to know more, so I went to my friend for a past-life regression. I saw myself as a young man in the shepherding community. I had my share of issues to resolve when I met Jesus. However, when I looked into his eyes and he saw me with the vision of Christ, many of the illusions just fell away.

I became involved in his work and began a healing journey. One day I came upon a crowd in a city courtyard. I saw that a mob was beating and tormenting Jesus. I was opposed to this treatment, but my efforts to stop it were futile. I couldn't remain there, so I walked far into the east. I sat on a rock for a long time and knew that I had a choice to make. I could go up into the hills to heal people in their dwellings or go back down into the city to mix it up with the energy of the mob.

I made my way back into town and bought bread. I remember eating it and fluctuating between feelings of anger and frustration about the situation and feelings of peace and certainty that all would be well. I went to my family's dwelling and they encouraged me to stay out of it and not to resist the status quo or I would be in danger. I'm not sure what choice I made. I couldn't go any further into the regression. Perhaps I did a bit of healing and a bit of resisting.

One psychic told me that I had become a healer during that lifetime. Unfortunately, I was crucified because my actions were met with resistance. I later met with clairvoyant energy workers who confirmed this. They also said that I had been stabbed with a spear through the throat for speaking out against authorities. The remarkable part was that although some of the pain from that experience was still in my energy field, we worked to remove it. From that day on, I was not hesitant to speak my truth. Fortunately, we now live in different times, and we have the freedom to speak out and share our truth without fear of reprisal.

My friend Anita Burns communicated with her guide Johar for me one day. He said, "Providing healing through the Christ force is your destiny." I am excited and honored to share it with others. It has made such a powerful and positive impact on my life. The Christ force energy creates a spiritual healing, and as you heal the Spirit, you heal the body. It brings a peace that surpasses understanding.

We are one. We are the body of Christ. As you open up to the awareness of this truth, you allow the energy of Christ to flow through you and out into the world to bless and heal. The Master Jesus is still actively assisting people to regain their connection with Spirit. Take advantage of this Divine assistance. You can also call upon other ascended masters and angels. You will be led to the remembrance of your own destiny, power, and divinity—your Christ self. I honor you for your role in the resurrection of consciousness that leads to atonement (at-one-ment) with our Creator.

Angel of Destiny Prayer

"Mother-Father God, I am willing to embrace my destiny. I have been given this lifetime to share my gifts and fulfill my purpose. I am ready to get to work and be on my path. I know you will guide me and offer me support. I am rededicating myself to sharing peace, love, and Christ force energy. It is my goal to reunite with my Creator in a state of perfection. I am grateful for opportunities to share my truth and help others to heal. And so it is."

Three ways that I will experience destiny in my life are . . .

1.

2.

3.

IDEAS:

1. Pursue your dreams and utilize your talents without concerns about impracticality, failure, or reprisal from others.

2. Dedicate an entire weekend to studying, praying, and communing with Christ. Pay attention to the inner guidance this creates regarding your life mission.

3. Pursue a love interest with great joy and determination, without fear or attachment to outcome.

nonresistance

What could you not accept, if you knew that
everything that happens, all events, past, present
and to come, are gently planned by One whose
only purpose is your good?

A COURSE IN MIRACLES

*Because you are starting to understand the importance of nonre-
sistance, an easy, gentle flow is moving through your life. Trying to
fight against circumstances tends to give them more power. When
you release investments in outcomes, you will see the miracles
manifest. When I was attending our earth school, I came across a
situation where I was challenged to make some changes in my perceptions and actions.*

*I was walking to the marketplace when two large men accosted
me. They told me that I should give them my coins. I remained
fairly calm in spite of this adversity and attempted to engage the
men in conversation. I told them that I needed to buy bread for my
baby sister who was not feeling well. She needed the nourishment
to regain her strength after a long illness.*

One of the men seemed to soften, but his partner was determined to pursue his course of action. I asked him why he needed the money. He told me that it was none of my business. Then he began to ask me questions about my family. I told him that my mother worked as a laundress and that she had seven children to feed. My father worked in the fields and did his best to supply his family with food and shelter. I told him that my father's employer might need more laborers. They both were interested in looking for work so that their current path might be made easier.

We walked into the village together and I introduced them to a shopkeeper and the landowner. The owner of the field said that he would be glad to hire them and would give them some provisions from the market. Later, the men turned to me in gratitude and said that they were thankful for this new opportunity. I felt that if I had resisted them when they approached, an entirely different outcome may have taken place.

I was silently praying and giving thanks to my inner guidance for leading me down the right path. I returned home with food for my sister who recovered from her illness. Because I was willing to set aside fear and go with the flow of the situation, I was protected and supported by the Universe. I had been taught that the Creator would always take care of me and I had an unquestioning faith about it.

You know that when you try to fight or attack, these lower energies feed upon themselves. You can see how people in a confrontation seem to ignite each other's anger. When you accept the qualities of your higher self, such as power, peace, understanding, compassion, and virtue, they will overcome lower vibrational energies. Your *life will begin to flow. I know that it is difficult to do this all of the time. As you put these principles into practice, it will become easier. You can always ask your guides to help you regulate your energy field. Much is being done in the unseen world to help you.*

If you fight against your life mission or purpose, you will find resistance. Know that Divine intelligence will lead you. You will know by inner sensations if you are doing the right thing. Because you have trusted in yourself, you will be shown. Give up control and manipulation and bring in acceptance. Your life will flow and you will be supported. Love and light, Jahallah.

As I was preparing to write this chapter, I kept experiencing little mishaps that provided me with opportunities to put nonresistance into practice. I am usually a very organized person, so I know where to find things around my house. However, within two weeks I misplaced my prescription sunglasses and other expensive items. I looked everywhere and became very frustrated.

My astrologer friend said that this had something to do with planets in retrograde, but that was no consolation. I found myself holding on to attachments to these objects. I *really* wanted them back. Even though these were not very traumatic incidents, they taught me to put my spiritual principles into practice. If we master acceptance of the small things that go wrong, it will be easier to cope with really difficult issues.

One of my friends told me a story about a crisis that her family experienced. One evening, her two younger brothers went out to a local bar. They frequented the place quite often and met some friends there. When they were ready to leave, one brother went outside to get the car. On the way out, he was struck on the head with a glass mug. Before he knew it, he was on the floor being stabbed. His brother ran out and saw him bleeding on the ground. Several men were standing over him, stabbing him repeatedly. Her brother tried his best to get the men off, but they turned and attacked him. He sustained minor injuries and his brother lost his vision in one eye.

After learning about the incident, my friend was overwhelmed with sorrow for her brothers. She was also filled with rage. The thought of the horrific attack haunted her. She wanted those men to be hurt in the way they hurt her brothers. A few weeks went by, and she realized that her desire to hurt those men was unjust. From a metaphysical perspective, she felt she had no right to judge the dynamics of karma between her brothers and their attackers.

She felt an overwhelming sense of compassion for everyone involved. She did not understand why it happened, but she did realize that there was a lesson to be learned. When we experience obstacles and hardships, we need to realize that they present opportunities to grow.

After shifting her perception of the trauma, she told me, "I choose to embrace the things I do not understand with love and compassion. My nonresistant attitude helped me to evolve into a more accepting spirit. I came to the realization that we need to take responsibility for the positive and the negative experiences in our lives."

As I finished typing this story, I gained renewed commitment to practicing nonresistance in my own life. It is remarkable how some people overcome major challenges. I felt like I was in the remedial school of nonresistance the week I wrote this chapter.

Since a lot of work goes into writing a book, I wanted to make sure all of my efforts were safeguarded from computer malfunctions. I downloaded copies of the chapters to floppy disks and even tape-recorded some material. I was copying two chapters one day and accidentally deleted them. It took me a few days to recover my composure. My friend and I laughed on the phone about my lack of acceptance over this little inconvenience. I have a little wooden statue that I call my "Computer Buddha." It sits over our monitor to remind me to remain calm and nonattached in these situations.

There is a saying that "what we resist, persists." I remember several occasions when I really wanted something and it remained out of reach until I let go of the need to attain it. I also noticed that my financial situation improved when I stopped worrying about it. Nobody ever said that the path to greater spiritual awareness would be easy. However, if we choose to develop certain qualities in our lives, the opportunities for growth will be there. For example, if you say, "God, make me more patient," you will probably be given situations that challenge your patience. The practice of nonresistance is difficult for many of us, but when we master it, we will gain freedom and peace of mind.

Angel of Nonresistance Prayer

"Mother-Father God, I know that you are guiding my life with a wise, gentle hand. I will not resist experiences that are designed to help me evolve and grow. I have a deep knowing that I am safe and that I have no need to attack, defend, or resist. Whenever I am faced with challenges, I will remember to choose love instead of fear. I am trusting in the Divine flow of life. And so it is."

Three ways that I will experience nonresistance in my life are . . .

1.

2.

3.

IDEAS:

1. When an unforeseen obstacle arises, do a breathing meditation until you release stress and constriction.

2. Experiment with a sensory deprivation flotation tank and let the salt water support you as you focus on your connection with God.

3. Say thank you for new challenges and bless them until you are no longer in pain about them.

perfect timing

Your passage through time and space is not at random. You cannot but be in the right place at the right time.

A COURSE IN MIRACLES

I would like to address the subject of perfect timing. There may be times when you try to push through an agenda and you find blocks in your way. This could be because your soul has another plan for you. At times, you will go through periods of rest. At other times, you will be active working on many projects. There is a need for both stillness and movement in your life. If you do not resist this flow, you will see a perfectly balanced order.

If you try to set your own time schedules, you might come across obstacles. When you follow your mind and not your heart, you may walk down many dead-end roads. However, when you accept that there is a higher intelligence guiding you along, the perfect meetings will take place at exactly the right time. When you open yourself up to acknowledging that there is a higher order to your life plan, you will become synchronized with it and you will eventually find what you are looking for.

Because you are never separate from the mind of God, you cannot become lost for long. Nobody becomes a lost soul. There will always be ways to return to the Light if the intention is there. You will soon find many who would ask you to be a way-shower. You may feel ill equipped to put yourself in the position of a teacher, but that is just your ego perception. We are all teachers and students on some level, and we have been sent here to assist each other.

While on earth, I was a guide that led people on treks across the desert. We needed to time our journeys so that harsh weather conditions would not impede our progress. We walked at night to avoid the strong rays of the sun. On one trip, our caravan wagon broke down and many of our provisions were lost. I had taken the route before and did not know of a place where we could replenish our supplies. I prayed hard while the others were sleeping. I was guided to take an alternate route, and we found an oasis. I marveled at our good fortune, and I knew deep within that all was in Divine order. We gathered around the water and gave thanks.

Imagine that you were on a sailing ship headed for a specific destination. A storm arose and you needed to veer off your course. If you persisted on your current path, you would have found yourself in harm's way. "Random" events are usually signposts that show you the direction to take. When you start to follow them, you will reach your destination by the safest, easiest route possible. You will sail down the current of life with the wind at your back and the angels by your side.

You will know when this is taking place by the ease and peace your choices bring. You can even weather the storms of fate easily when you put your perceptions in alignment with the One Who Knows. Break through the patterns of resistance that impede you from hearing my voice. Trying to swim against the tide will only tire you out. There is no need to weary yourselves, dear ones. We see many caught in a whirlwind of frenetic activity, just to stay afloat. They feel like they are drowning and that they must continue to struggle, but this is not the case.

Your Mother/Father will buoy you up and take you safely to shore. It is fine for you to rest a while in God's loving embrace. Bask in the warmth of the sun and soak up the regenerating energy of the earth. If you are sincere in your desire to be at one with Creation, the timing will be right for you and you will find your way again. Peaceful journeys, Jahallah.

My life has been filled with incidents that were timed perfectly. I didn't always recognize them because I had to venture through the obstacles before I reached my goals. I found a lovely home and rewarding career by staying true to myself and being patient. I can't say that I was always confident and sure of God's guidance, but it is getting easier as time passes.

I had wanted to attend an angel therapy practitioner course with Dr. Doreen Virtue for several years. I was determined to give myself that experience, and I registered for a fall course in Laguna Beach, California. When it was time to pay for the program, I had the money. I knew it would be a positive step in my spiritual growth. I wasn't disappointed. It was a wonderful week, and I gained many tools that strengthened my healing and intuitive counseling abilities.

When I walked into the meeting room on the first day, I knew that I was exactly where I was supposed to be. It brought tears to my eyes to see so many people dedicated to spiritual growth and healing. I usually avoid being in large groups, but the energy was high and the people were very loving. It felt like a family reunion. It was wonderful to meet other lightworkers who spoke my language. I was encouraged on my path and given insights about the publication of my book.

At the same time that I was enjoying many synchronicities in my career, my best friend, Cyndi Butler, was finding out how perfect timing occurred when she followed her heart. Cyndi and I had known each other for twenty years. We had gone through some lean times together, and we helped bolster each other up when we faced challenges. We both knew about affirmations, positive thinking, and manifestation. We worked at putting those concepts into practical application and were amazed by the results.

Cyndi moved to Oregon to start a new life and be near her family. She found a beautiful home across the street from a recreation center for her children. I was thrilled when she landed a good-paying marketing position that offered benefits and a company car. Although she had many talents in this area, it wasn't really her passion. Since childhood, she had been a psychic and a medium; however, some frightening experiences caused her to shut down her gifts.

When she was finally ready to utilize her abilities, opportunities to do this work flooded toward her. She gave a sample reading to a friend and was immediately booked for a party. She worked for over six hours straight and received a very generous compensation. She was told afterward that she had changed people's lives and helped them to heal and grow.

The contacts she made at this event became good customers and told their friends about her work. I have heard many stories of people creating successful lives by following their hearts. I have learned not to worry or rush as much because I know that the dynamic of perfect timing is active in my life. It is amazing to see how the Universe supports us when we make Spirit our focus.

Angel of Perfect Timing Prayer

"Mother-Father God, I have no need to worry or struggle because my life is being guided by Divine intelligence. All will unfold according to a perfect plan. I will be led to people and situations that provide me with an abundant life. Because I am not afraid, my vision is not clouded. I will see opportunities to create the life of my dreams and act at the perfect time. I savor the beauty in each moment and embrace the gifts of the present. And so it is."

Three ways that I will experience perfect timing in my life
are . . .

1.

2.

3.

IDEAS:

1. Put away watches and clocks for a day with the knowledge that each event will be timed perfectly.

2. Rent an educational video about the gestation and birth
   of a butterfly and observe the way nature does not rush
   creation.

3. Say a prayer of thanks to the Universe for the day your
   beloved crossed your path (this could be a mate, spiritual teacher, or even a cherished pet).

sanctuary

> There is a place in you where there is perfect
> peace. There is a place in you where nothing is
> impossible. There is a place in you where the
> strength of God abides.
>
> A COURSE IN MIRACLES

*What is a sanctuary? It is a place where you can be free of the
concerns of the outer world. It could be a place secluded in nature.
It could be a small private space where you go for peace and renewal. I'd like to direct you to the sanctuary within yourself. You
can be in the midst of activity and seeming chaos, yet go within at
any time and access your place of refuge.*

*Relax and go within now, perhaps to the center of your head.
Designate that spot as yours alone. Picture it in any manner that
brings comfort to you. You might enjoy a forest clearing with a
stream. You might like a deserted beach with the sun warming your
skin. You might like a beautiful room with a comfortable chair.
Make yourself at home in your private place.*

There are no concerns or worries that can infiltrate the bubble of protection surrounding you. You are perfectly safe and free from harm. You might want to have a conversation with your Creator or your higher self. Discuss the areas of your life in which you would like peace. See those situations being healed in your mind's eye. Accept the peace and bask in its glow.

Go into silent meditation. If you find your mind interjecting, comfort it briefly like a small child and return to the quiet that you have created. When you are finished, give yourself a cue, such as a word or feeling, that will help you return to this state at any time. If you are caught up in daily stress, remind yourself of the cue and generate the feeling of sanctuary again. It is possible to experience tranquility at all times. Your mind can come up with many arguments disputing this, but it does not change the fact that the only constant thing in the universe is the love of God.

The other experiences are just temporary. With love, all things can be transformed and healed. Whenever you feel as though the worries of the world are upon you, take a deep breath and say, "I choose peace instead of this." It may take a bit of practice to convince yourself of this truth. Sometimes people stubbornly hold onto their discontent because it is familiar. As you continue to practice being in the present moment and accepting peace, those patterns will be eliminated.

A wildlife sanctuary is a place where animals can live without the risk of predators. Many people go about their lives in fear for their own safety. They see violent images of attack all around them and begin to believe the world is unsafe. These beliefs are perpetuated by much of the media, and the fear spreads. Remember that like attracts like. If you believe there is danger around you, it may manifest. Your safety lies in your belief that you are safe.

If you need extra encouragement, call upon your guides and angels. Each human being can create a protective sphere of energy that keeps them safe from harm. You can have sanctuary in every moment of your life, even while passing through ghetto streets or war zones. There is no reason for you to be afraid. Your spirit is eternal and there is no risk of annihilation. You are an irreplaceable part of the One.

Your locks, weapons, and security devices are but talismans used to support your superstitious beliefs. They do not provide you with safety. It is your birthright to be invincible. If you had even a small understanding of the love that the Creator has for you, there would be no more doubts.

If you would, return to the place of sanctuary that you created earlier. Picture a beautiful fountain in the center, spraying up and washing away all concerns and limiting beliefs. This flow of life-giving essence is never ending, and it is available to you at all times. Drink of its sweetness and refresh yourself. Know that as you allow yourself to accept this gift, it will increase. You can then become an instrument of peace to others and help them to remember that they are safe. When people are in your presence, they will find sanctuary as this flow of energy washes over and renews them.

When I was a young man, my friends and I went to a celebration. There were many people at this gathering, and the revelry turned into mischief. People were acting out and causing disruption.

This triggered the anger of others and a brawl ensued. A government official came out to see if he could restore order. He was met by hostility, yet he remained calm. He didn't threaten or overwhelm with force, but stayed firm in his expectations. He looked the mischief-makers in the eye and reminded them of who they really were. He saw past the temporary situation and saw their God selves. Everyone started to calm down and peace was returned to the village.

Whenever outside circumstances tempt you to lose your peace, go within to your place of sanctuary. Remind yourself of what is true. You will never be alone and you are always protected. You have help from the spiritual realms. Pray to God and ask that you will be able to see this clearly. Ask for assistance from your guides and angels. Immerse yourself in the river of life and let go of the fear. You are safe, Jahallah.

A friend and I went to a lecture about crystal children. She was very dedicated to raising her psychic son in a supportive environment and was hoping to gain insights from this workshop. We listened to the speaker tell about the many wonderful aspects of raising a crystal child. These children are born with their spiritual gifts intact and help to raise the consciousness of the planet. During the question and answer period, my friend raised her hand and told us about the challenges she had encountered. Her home had been bombarded with lower vibrational entities and discarnate spirits that troubled her little boy. Her story was so heartfelt and sincere that the audience broke out into tears and applause. The speaker gave her tools for clearing and sealing energy fields. She encouraged my friend to focus on the positive aspects of her situation.

Others in the audience told about difficult times they had with their children. A few of them had life-threatening diseases and were misdiagnosed as autistic. There was one man who was lost in a maze of therapies for his child and at a loss about how to proceed. This teacher usually focuses on the fact that lightworkers are divinely protected and can live a life filled with ease and abundance. However, she felt she needed to caution the man that his family had created such light that the dark side had made an effort to break it apart. She did advise, however, that if he followed his heart and stayed true to his spiritual connection, everything would be fine.

On the drive home, my friend and I discussed the challenges of being on this path. She was glad that the "dark issues" were addressed instead of being hidden behind platitudes. She said, "You have to write about both sides in your book in order to provide a true picture of the world." We discussed the robberies we had experienced and tried to make sense of all the chaos on the planet. I told her that I had a renewed conviction that my world was safe and that I would be protected.

Granted, there are beings that are up to no good, but the light will always shine away the darkness. I do think that our angels and guides were still on the scene during our hardships, preventing even greater damage from taking place. Even though my friend's son had been frightened by dark spirits, the Universe provided healers and teachers to offer immediate help. When I was challenged by a similar situation, I was stunned by the outcome.

When my daughter Briana was having a difficult time adjusting to a school with many outbreaks of violence, we tried to find a place that would offer a more positive environment. She was sad, but I was beside myself with grief. I went into fear and panic for some reason. I put all of my energy into finding a school where she felt safe and secure. We hit a few roadblocks and finally decided to homeschool for six months. Her brother Chris joined us because he was also unhappy in the toxic and violent atmosphere.

It was not an easy road, but I think it strengthened our family ties. I brought the kids to a psychic fair where my friend was working. She dealt a few cards and had a stricken look on her face. She said, "Amy, I see dark entities invading your energy field. But don't become alarmed because there is still a ray of light shining through." She felt the need for backup from a couple of women with whom she had worked in the past. I was a little unnerved because my psychic readings were usually about love and light.

As I sat in front of them, I didn't understand what was going on. They all saw the same thing—"spiders" were covering me and they could barely see my true colors underneath. I was hesitant to believe it because I never had exposure to the dark side. I gasped out loud as a woman I had never met before said, "The entities were able to get into your space because there was a tear in your aura caused by the fear you had over your daughter's school situation." My mouth dropped open. It was true. I usually wasn't a fearful person, but that experience threw me off balance for some inexplicable reason.

The good news was that these psychic women kicked butt and took no prisoners. They told those creepy crawlers to make a swift retreat if they didn't want trouble. They all seemed happy with the results of their work and told me that I should feel much lighter and able to manifest what I really wanted more easily.

My point is that even lightworkers and crystal people can face challenges, but they are always overcome with wisdom and light. Using clearing and protection tools will eliminate most problems. I suggest calling upon Archangel Michael to cut negative energy chords and to "vacuum out" any unwanted visitors. You can also surround yourself in white and colored light as a protective shield.

The most important thing we can do is to avoid going into a space of fear and vulnerability. That only breaks down our defenses. Spirit will provide you with the perfect teachers and helpers as well. All you have to do is ask and be willing to receive assistance. We can always find sanctuary by going within and creating a strong connection with the Divine. Go to your special place often so that when upset occurs, you will quickly be able to regain your peace.

Angel of Sanctuary Prayer

"Mother-Father God, I am ready to accept the peace and sanctuary that is always available to me. I am grateful that I live in a world filled with love and acceptance. I let go of worries and access the assistance of my spiritual helpers. I am secure in knowing that there is no way I can be separate from my Creator. When I forget this, I will go within for refuge. As I strengthen my connection to the Divine, this will become easier. I choose to create heaven on earth. And so it is."

Three ways that I will experience sanctuary in my life are . . .

1.

2.

3.

IDEAS:

1. Participate in a silent meditation retreat at a spiritual center, such as the Self Realization Fellowship.

2. Take a hike in a wildlife sanctuary and make a financial contribution to its preservation.

3. Record a guided meditation for yourself, envisioning a visit to an idyllic place designed specifically for inner solace and rejuvenation.

transformation

When a mind has only light it knows only light,
its own radiance shines all around it, and extends
out into the darkness of other minds, transforming
them into majesty.

A COURSE IN MIRACLES

*You know that when you feel out of sorts, it is useful to take an in-
ventory of your inner emotions and your external life situation.
What issues might be contributing to your feelings of discomfort?
The next step in your journey is transformation of these situations.
You have been exploring many aspects of your life and diligently
making progress toward change. The seeds have been planted, and
you will soon start to bloom into a new creation.*

*Because you are trying to understand this process from the scope
of knowledge you already have, you may not realize how profound
this shift is going to be. You will awaken each morning in sheer bliss
as you will breathe in life. Your daily existence won't seem like a
chore, but a choreographed dance of joy. As you embrace your role*

in the master plan, you will have a strong sense that all is well in your world.

Feel the angel blessings falling like raindrops to revive and sustain you. Reach your roots into Mother Earth and soak in her nurturing energy. Your cosmic Creator is shining his light down upon you to help you radiate your essence outward. If you only knew how many unseen forces were supporting you along the journey, you would never be afraid.

Whenever you try to fit round pegs into square holes, frustration will arise. Call to mind any areas of your life where you are finding resistance, and focus love on them. Love is a transforming energy. It can change the shape of the peg or the hole so that union will take place.

I remember a time when I was swimming in the ocean. I was drifting out to sea in a strong current. I saw a rock island in the distance and tried to reach it. I finally gained refuge on this desolate outcropping. There was nothing there but crabs and urchins. Occasionally seagulls would rest from their flights. "Well," I thought to myself, "this stopping place is fine to rest on for a while, but it is not getting me any closer to my desired destination."

I used the time to pray and meditate and gain inner strength. I was inspired to try a different route to reach the shore that wouldn't put me into direct competition with the current. It took every bit of stamina that I had, but I made it to land. The sense of overwhelming gratitude I felt upon reaching the beach encompassed every cell in my body. I was vibrating with joy.

Sometimes our biggest challenges are our means of greatest transformation. They teach us which choices lead to hardship and *which choices lead to peace. Your perseverance will pay off. I know that you will try to find your way home, no matter what the obstacles. It is a journey without distance. Your Creator had never left you, but awaits your remembrance.*

When your awakening takes place, your entire existence will be transformed into heaven on earth. The things of the world will provide you with minor amusements, but your real satisfaction will come from your connection to Spirit. Think of the great spiritual teachers throughout history. They did not always have an easy road to walk, but their lives greatly impacted the transformation of consciousness on the planet. I know that each of you will continue to do your best to help each other to grow. We are all in this together, creating a web of love. Your space in heaven is awaiting your return. You are irreplaceable in the mind of God. Countless blessings, Jahallah.

I took a break for a few months during the writing of this book. My kids were out of school for the summer and I didn't feel quite prepared to tackle such lofty subjects as "transformation" and "enlightenment." When I finally sat back down at my keyboard, I wrote two sentences and reached for my thesaurus. Tucked away behind it was a quote about the promises we can make to ourselves to create what we want in life. I can't remember where I originally found the material, but it was a reminder from Spirit of what is meant by transformation. It reminded me to release the limits I had created for myself and move into my full potential.

I felt that I needed a "power place" journey to gear up for the completion of the book. I suggested a family vacation to Mount Shasta. My best friend's sister was going to be singing in Shasta County and I thought it would be a good weekend to make the trip. My friend was going to drive down from Oregon and meet me in Shasta. Since my husband had planned a weekend motorcycle-riding trip with the boys and my daughter was scheduled to attend an animal show at a local fairgrounds, I headed out by myself.

I read books about Mount Shasta before my trip, envisioning metaphysical marvels, such as meeting Lemurians that are said to dwell inside the mountain on the fifth dimension. I wondered if I would have any alien encounters or meet an ascended master. I hoped I would have a transformational experience that would make excellent material for the conclusion of the book. My experience wasn't very exotic or supernatural, but I think I understood what Spirit was trying to communicate.

I loved being in the mountains, enjoying the energy of the trees and breathing the fresh air. I felt connected with the Divine as I walked. I spent the first afternoon exploring the area. As I drove up the mountain, many woodland creatures ran across my path. Squirrels, chipmunks, and field mice scampered in front of my car. The Native Americans pay attention to encounters with animals and the messages they have to share. I have been told by a discarnate named Sun Dancer that I have many power animals from the forest. I researched the meanings of these encounters and I found that they were reminders to do my spiritual work and communicate my truth.

I have been told that the indigenous people looked to the land as their bible, gathering messages and insights from their natural surroundings. I seated myself on a rock just below the summit of the mountain. In the middle of summer, there were still patches of snow on the peak. I started to gaze at the snow and rock formations, looking for pictures.

One patch definitely resembled the Virgin Mary surrounded by a host of angels. She wore robes and her hands were outstretched. She appeared to be sending out comfort and inspiration. This was significant to me because books about Mary have made a powerful impact on my life. I hiked the mountain and enjoyed the beauty all around me. In the evening, I returned to my quiet little bungalow and had a peaceful night's rest.

The next morning, I went on a "vortex tour" and I was happy to talk with people who were very knowledgeable and insightful. We discussed the mythology of the mountain and the energies of nature. My friend had experienced personal challenges and travel delays and was unable to join us for the tour. As we were discussing this, a wounded hawk crossed our path. The psychic tour guide felt that this was a message for my friend. She was a very powerful being, but her wounds had prevented her from utilizing her full potential.

We did a meditation at a medicine wheel and drank from a natural spring in a lovely meadow. We hiked to a waterfall and enjoyed the uplifting energy. After lunch, I sat down with the guide and we discussed my life and future. Jahallah came through and indicated that he was "pulling me along" in order to complete the book. He was grateful for the work that I had put into it and said he would move on after our assignment was completed. I was told that publication and promotion would flow smoothly.

There was one thing that I needed to address, however, in order for me to regain my power. I needed to communicate with and eliminate the negative self-talk from my shadow self. My counselor said that the shadow self is the part of us that feels wrong, wounded, or incomplete. At workshops addressing such issues, I usually step outside when things get too touchy-feely. I have never been drawn to exploring inner children, gazing into a stranger's eyes, or saying kooky affirmations. However, I had traveled over six hundred miles to transform and I was willing to do what it took.

We listened to what the wounded aspect of me had to say. "Where do I fit in? When I share my truth, I get shut down. I don't trust that the Universe will provide for me because the past has been difficult. I am not good enough to attract quality relationships into my life. If I am going to fail, why should I try? Maybe I just wasn't meant to succeed."

Then it was time to send a beam of love from my heart into my shadow's heart. It was time to show her that there is another way of being. I realized that it takes way too much effort to hold on to limiting beliefs. We brought in the violet flame to transmute the energy into its original essence of love and light. I was then ready to bring in the goddess aspect of my higher self. The message from my higher self was, "If we do more of what we love, we will be successful. We will have a circle of women that provides us with support on our journey. We are committed to having a wonderful life and helping others do the same."

As I finished typing this chapter, I was ready to transform and do things differently. I made myself the promise to accept myself unconditionally, to not demand perfection, and to give myself the credit I deserve. I would be my own best friend and utilize my God-given talent to make a positive contribution to the world. I know that I have grown on this journey toward enlightenment. I wake up most days feeling overjoyed and grateful for my wonderful life. That has not always been the case, so I know from firsthand experience that when we learn spiritual principles and apply them to our lives, we will be transformed.

Angel of Transformation Prayer

"Mother-Father God, I am ready to be transformed.
I have experienced many aspects of a process that is
leading me to my desired destination. I will not arrive
as the same person who started the journey. I have
newfound hope, love, joy, and compassion as a result
of my experiences. I am ready to take the final step
and find union with my Creator. I will release anything that is blocking my awareness of love's presence.
And so it is."

Three ways that I will experience transformation in my life are . . .

1.

2.

3.

IDEAS:

1. Treat yourself to an energy healing with crystals, essential oils, and/or vibrational healing tools.

2. Work with a friend or counselor to identify limiting beliefs and replace them with truth.

3. Visit a metaphysical bookstore and purchase products and information for spiritual growth.

enlightenment

Man is free at the moment he wishes to be.

VOLTAIRE

Dear one, welcome to this new dimension of reality where there is only love and peace. You have taken a journey that has led you to the remembrance of your true self. Translating my thoughts into words has been a process of connecting more strongly with truth. Take notes daily from your Higher Guidance to help you solve personal issues as they arise.

The only thing that is different about an enlightened person is that he recognizes his own divinity and the divinity of everyone else. Usually, when you reach this stage of development, ego concerns have little relevance. Your greatest passion is to be of service and bring light to the world. Let go of preconceived ideas about how this state should look and feel. You will know it and you will be in bliss. Every path is different, but the destination is the same. They all lead to remembrance.

When you remember the power and gifts within you, they will manifest into the physical realms. Because you have chosen to be an instrument of love, these abilities will become apparent soon. Have you noticed that time seems to be "flying by"? You are moving very quickly in your evolution, so the time for dragging your feet and procrastinating is over. Many of you have experienced a "cosmic kick in the pants" to get you back on your spiritual paths. Eliminate the drama by saying "yes" to Spirit in this moment. Be willing to fulfill your mission.

Understand that you are here to be a way-shower. Don't be concerned if you have lost your road map and feel that you are blindly stumbling along. As long as you move forward, your destination will be reached. Others will follow your example. Tap into the guidance of ascended masters such as Jesus, Mary, Yogananda, Buddha, Quan Yin, and others. Research the teachings of each master and you will find the ones that you resonate with. They have dedicated themselves to helping humans make a transition in consciousness. You would be thwarting their Divine purpose if you didn't accept their help.

I have graduated from the earth school, yet it is my great pleasure to make contacts with mankind in order to uplift and encourage. The last thing that I did in my final incarnation was to thank my teachers for the role they played in my transformation. Love, generosity, and wisdom are invaluable gifts that we share with one another. We all have a unique role to fulfill in the Divine plan. Creation would be incomplete without your contribution, so please step forward and make it.

Take action daily toward reawakening Spirit in your life. I know that people get sidetracked easily with mundane concerns, but if you dedicate yourself to putting aside a certain amount of time each day for God, you won't be disappointed with the payoff. You will find more peace and contentment and greater clarity. If you have lost enthusiasm for this earthly game, connecting with your higher self will motivate you to move forward. Prayer and meditation are like tonics to the soul. Singing, chanting, and dancing can also inspire you. Begin each day with a realization that you are a beloved child of God.

When nothing else matters except for your union with the Source, you will have reached your goal. When you reach that state, there will be no more questioning, no more striving, no more struggling. You will exist in the present moment and know that all is well. Accept your enlightened nature. I Am, Jahallah.

As I was typing the final message from Jahallah, I was distracted for a moment and stopped writing. My computer made a strange sound and I looked at the screen. There was a flashing exclamation point after the sentence "Love, generosity, and wisdom are invaluable gifts that we share with one another." That was a powerful message for me. I do think that this project was designed to be a motivational tool for people to take steps toward these qualities.

I was dragging my feet about writing the last chapter because I felt it needed to make a powerful impact. I lay in bed, postponing the inevitable, when I glanced at the clock. It was 9:11, the signal for me that it was "time to get to work." I got the message and prepared myself to take divinely inspired action that might make a positive difference in people's lives. Besides writing this book, I thought of ways that I might share love with others. I thought about being more generous with my time and resources. I stopped to give thanks for the wise teachers that have shared their truth with me.

I wrote what I thought were some pretty uplifting paragraphs for this topic, when my computer froze up. It had happened before, and I lost all of my unsaved material. I stared in shock at the computer screen. What on earth was Spirit trying to teach me by this episode? How was I to recreate my lost work?

I turned the computer on and off a few times and tried to find ways to retrieve the lost text. I finally gave up because it was getting late. I figured that if I had made it to chapter 33, I must have learned something about nonattachment in the process. I told myself that I wasn't going to get upset about it. I went to bed that night and tried to block out all of those little regrets: "What did I write in those paragraphs? What could I possibly have to say tomorrow?"

I had to get some sleep, and I began to relax as the message came to me: "We are born again in each moment. The past no longer exists. There will always be enough to sustain you in the present moment. There are no right or wrong answers. There are as many paths to God as there are people who walk them. You will find your own way."

The next morning I did my Web site work for the store, answered e-mails, and did some household chores. I steered clear of the word processor, not knowing how to begin. I opted for eating a slice of German chocolate cake and watching a comedy video instead of writing. The laughter and the chocolate made me feel better. When my mood had improved, I was ready to proceed. I vowed not to take life so seriously.

I called to mind my favorite *Course in Miracles* quote: "The peace of God is my one goal; the aim of all my living here, the end I seek, my purpose and my function and my life." I returned to the computer and turned it on again. I was incredulous as I looked at the bottom of the screen. There was my file "Chapter 33 Enlightenment" with many of the changes I had made. I felt angel bumps and gave a smile of gratitude. I glanced at the "Computer Buddha" above my monitor and acknowledged the lesson.

The Buddha had a lot to say about enlightenment: "There are two mistakes one can make along the road to truth . . . not going all the way and not starting. . . . No one saves us but ourselves. No one can and no one may. We ourselves must walk the path. . . . The greatest gift is to give people your enlightenment, to share it."

I don't know too much about the traditional beliefs regarding enlightenment, but I do know that there is a Buddhist path of service. Since I haven't been too successful with disciplines such as breathing, meditation, and yoga, I think I will try this one on for size. It seems easy enough. Helping people comes naturally to me. I don't think this implies doing things for others that they can do for themselves. If you try to "fix" other people's lives, you may be slowing down their progress. Everyone has to figure things out for themselves, learn the lessons, and shift in consciousness.

To me, being of service means empowering others to reach their potential. In order to do this we must do our own inner work. As we raise our vibrations, we will help others by the dynamics of resonance. Traditional dogma tells us that Jesus was sent here to "save" us. Perhaps this really means that masters, such as Jesus, have raised their energy fields to such a level that they are able to transmute lower vibrational energies. It is very healing to merge with a master's loving presence.

Jesus also taught by example and inspired others to take a higher path. People who are enlightened are also able to make a positive impact on social situations that are not serving the good of mankind. History has not been too kind to these leaders, but I envision a kinder and gentler future. I really believe that the "second coming" will take place when humans access their Christ selves and we can live in a heavenly paradise on earth.

When I started this book, my channeling teacher brought through my guides. I was told that there were others in Spirit who were waiting to work with me and that I was to write a series of books. As I neared the end of my first project, I felt the need to write more about the spiritual journey. Thirty-three more topics came to me, including forgiveness, compassion, diversity, honesty, transcendence, hope, reverence, and miracles. There was so much more for me to explore.

I think that enlightenment can be a process that sometimes takes many lifetimes to achieve. I also believe that it can happen in an instant. When we are ready to let go of all of the blocks to love's presence, we will find it. If we make the effort to become self-aware in small ways, we will live consciously. Eventually, we will all return to our original state of perfection and communion with God. If we take a step closer each day, we will inevitably reach our destination.

Angel of Enlightenment Prayer

"Mother-Father God, enlightenment is a state of non-separation. I ask that I realize my oneness with all creation and that I help others to realize this truth. I know that life will be filled with bliss and harmony when all blocks to this realization are removed. Please fill me with peace now and help me to remember the perfection in which I was created. Shine your bright light of awareness upon me so that I may see clearly and know that I am love. And so it is."

One way that I will experience enlightenment in my life is . . .
1. Be who I am.

Free Magazine

Read unique articles by Llewellyn authors, recommendations by experts, and information on new releases. To receive a **free** copy of Llewellyn's consumer magazine, *New Worlds of Mind & Spirit,* simply call 1-877-NEW-WRLD or visit our website at www.llewellyn.com and click on *New Worlds.*

LLEWELLYN ORDERING INFORMATION

Order Online:
Visit our website at www.llewellyn.com, select your books, and order them on our secure server.

Order by Phone:
- Call toll-free within the U.S. at 1-877-NEW-WRLD (1-877-639-9753). Call toll-free within Canada at 1-866-NEW-WRLD (1-866-639-9753)
- We accept VISA, MasterCard, and American Express

Order by Mail:
Send the full price of your order (MN residents add 7% sales tax) in U.S. funds, plus postage & handling to:
Llewellyn Worldwide
2143 Wooddale Drive, Dept. 0-7387-0896-8
Woodbury, Minnesota 55125-2989, U.S.A.

Postage & Handling:

Standard (U.S., Mexico, & Canada). If your order is:
$49.99 and under, add $3.00
$50.00 and over, FREE STANDARD SHIPPING

AK, HI, PR: $15.00 for one book plus $1.00 for each additional book.

International Orders (airmail only):
$16.00 for one book plus $3.00 for each additional book

Orders are processed within 2 business days.
Please allow for normal shipping time. Postage and handling rates subject to change.

Discover Your Spiritual Life
Illuminate Your Soul's Path

ELIZABETH OWENS

Some are led to the spiritual path by a mystical experience, by a tragic life circumstance, or by nagging feelings of discontent. Whatever the reason, you need a road map or guide to assist you along the way. Spiritualist medium Elizabeth Owens gives you the tools to connect with that higher guidance that, she says, already resides within yourself.

Learn a life-changing method for handling problems and disappointments. Discover effective ways to meditate, pray, create affirmations, forgive those who have hurt you, and practice gratitude. Process painful emotions and thoughts quickly through the art of becoming a balanced observer.

0-7387-0423-7
264 pp., 5³⁄₁₆ x 8 $12.95

Spiritual Fitness

Embrace Your Soul, Transform Your Life

NANCY MRAMOR, PH.D.

This is self-transformation that begins with the spirit. On our eternal quest for self-improvement—trying to attain beauty, love, or health—there is a vital area often overlooked: our spiritual well-being. Psychologist Dr. Nancy Mramor takes readers on a journey of self-transformation that begins with the spirit.

Spiritual Fitness provides a curriculum for life that nourishes the spiritual self and builds a strong connection to the Divine. This self-directed program encourages spiritual awareness and growth through self-exploration and exercises involving meditation, prayer, visualization, breathing, music, and color. An inspirational quote begins each chapter. The author also shares personal accounts of her own mystical experiences—including her triumphant battle with cancer—and other irrefutable evidence of the spirit's infinite power.

0-7387-0640-X
240 pp., 5¾₆ x 8 $14.95

Transformative Meditation

Personal & Group Practice to Access
Realms of Consciousness

GAYLE CLAYTON

Never underestimate the power of a small group of conscious, committed individuals to change the world. As humanity grows ever more complex, we need to balance technological advances with an evolution of higher consciousness. One way to do that is through group or collective meditation.

This system of meditation creates a single identity that transforms the individuals, the group, and later, the world. Select groups and teachers have already incorporated collective meditation into successful practice. Now, *Transformative Meditation* introduces this system to everyone. It presents an overview of meditation systems, explores the various levels of transformative meditation, and teaches you how to move the group to upper astral planes, how to chant to create a higher identity, and how to increase moments of mystical awareness.

0-7387-0502-0
216 pp., 6 x 9   **$12.95**

Choosing Joy, Creating Abundance
Practical Tools for Manifesting Your Desires
ELLEN PETERSON

Millions of people give up on their dreams every day. They believe success is impossible without a stroke of luck, such as winning the lottery. *Choosing Joy, Creating Abundance* offers a ray of sunshine to those who have lost all hope in personal prosperity.

Offering a psychological and spiritual perspective on prosperous living, psychotherapist Ellen Peterson explores the practical dimensions of abundance. She helps readers define their ideas of personal success and overcome the hidden obstacles that often hinder prosperity. Her empowering words, sensible advice, and personal stories illustrate that inner peace and contentment are within everyone's grasp.

0-7387-0543-8
216 pp., 6 x 9 $12.95

To order, call 1-877-NEW-WRLD
Prices subject to change without notice

To Write to the Author

If you wish to contact the author or would like more information about this book, please write to the author in care of Llewellyn Worldwide and we will forward your request. Both the author and publisher appreciate hearing from you and learning of your enjoyment of this book and how it has helped you. Llewellyn Worldwide cannot guarantee that every letter written to the author can be answered, but all will be forwarded. Please write to:

Amy Elizabeth Garcia
℅ Llewellyn Worldwide
2143 Wooddale Drive, Dept. 0-7387-0896-8
Woodbury, MN 55125-2989, U.S.A.

Please enclose a self-addressed stamped envelope for reply,
or $1.00 to cover costs. If outside U.S.A., enclose
international postal reply coupon.

Many of Llewellyn's authors have websites with additional information and resources. For more information, please visit our website at:

http://www.llewellyn.com